MORTALLY WOUNDED

STORIES OF SOUL PAIN,
DEATH, AND HEALING

MICHAEL KEARNEY, M.D.

for Christine and Roberto
with thanks
and all good wishes,

Michael

A TOUCHSTONE BOOK
Published by Simon & Schuster

TOUCHSTONE
Rockefeller Center
1230 Avenue of the Americas
New York, NY 10020

Originally published in Ireland by Marino Books

First Touchstone Edition 1997

TOUCHSTONE and colophon are registered trademarks
of Simon & Schuster Inc.

DESIGNED BY ERICH HOBBING

Manufactured in the United States of America

1 3 5 7 9 10 8 6 4 2

The Library of Congress has cataloged the Scribner edition as follows:
Kearney, Michael, M.D.
Mortally wounded : stories of soul pain, death, and healing / Michael Kearney.
p.   cm.
Includes bibliographical references.
1. Hospice care—Psychological aspects. 2. Spiritual healing. 3. Death—Religious
aspects—Christianity. 4. Death—Psychological aspects. I. Title.
R726.8.K43   1996
155.9'37—dc20   96-22913
CIP

ISBN 0-684-83220-8
ISBN 0-684-83537-1 (Pbk)

For permission to reproduce copyright material, the publishers are grateful to the following: R. S. Thomas for "This to Do" and an extract from "Here," from the Oxford
University Press edition of *Selected Poems 1946–1968*.

For Marian

Healing

I am not a mechanism, an assembly of various sections.
And it is not because the mechanism is working wrongly,
    that I am ill.
I am ill because of wounds to the soul, to the deep emo-
    tional self
and the wounds to the soul take a long, long time,
    only time can help
and patience, and a certain difficult repentance
long, difficult repentance, realisation of life's mistake,
    and the freeing oneself
from the endless repetition of the mistake
which mankind at large has chosen to sanctify.

D. H. Lawrence

Contents

CONTENTS

PART 4: DEPTH WORK

Acknowledgments

First, I want to thank my wife, Marian. She has encouraged me throughout this project and helped me keep my feet on the ground. I also want to thank my wonderful daughters, Mary Anna, Claire, and Ruth, for their visits of curiosity, distraction, and humor while I was wrestling with my word processor in the basement.

There are many individuals who have given me help in a variety of ways, and I am indebted to Cicely Saunders, Tom West, Mary Baines, Balfour Mount, Anna Farmar, Mary Condren, Patrick Nolan, Anne Hayes, Richard Kearney, Jonathan Williams, Jo O'Donoghue, Micheál O'Regan, Marych O'Sullivan, and Patricia Skar. I am grateful also to Bernard and Mary Loughlin of the Tyrone Guthrie Centre in Annaghmakerrig and the Columban Sisters at Maheramore, County Wicklow, for their hospitality.

For editorial reasons what should sometimes read "we" in the stories that follow has been simplified to "I." However, the type of work with people close to death that I write of here is possible only as teamwork, and I want to express my appreciation and gratitude to the palliative care teams I work with at Our Lady's Hospice and St. Vincent's Hospital in Dublin.

I acknowledge an enormous debt to James Hillman, whose thinking has inspired me and led me into depth and is at the very core of the book. His personal encouragement at the early stages of my writing meant a lot to me. I want to thank Sri Madhava Ashish, whose unexpected enthusiasm from afar helped me to believe in the value of this project, Melanie Reinhart for her wonderful book on Chiron, and Robert Bly for his powerful poetic translations.

Finally, I acknowledge my coauthors Jackie, Emma, Bill, Sean, Eamonn, Dara, Frank, Bairbre, Anne, and James. I am very grateful to them and to their families for permission to tell their stories, which form the heart and soul of the book. I count myself lucky to have had such guides and mentors along the way.

Foreword

Those of us who have spent time in the company of people with mortal illness have learned from them that we are always challenged to know more and to help more effectively but, above all, to listen. Sometimes there will be no answers to give to those in apparently desperate situations, and we find ourselves with nothing to offer but silent attention. People who are experiencing "soul pain," as Michael Kearney describes it, bring us face to face not only with their need but with our own. A feeling of helplessness may urge us to withdraw or to escape into a zealous hyperactivity which can well exacerbate the patient's suffering. There is also a very real danger that the caregiver's despair of ever changing the situation may suggest the solution of physician-assisted suicide or euthanasia as practiced in Holland.

If we can resist these negative reactions and keep coming back, even those without the skills described here can reach a place of mutual growth. Much "soul pain" is reached and healed by the way care is carried out. Most people, given space by recognition of their worth as unique individuals accompanied by the multidisciplinary approach of effective palliative care, will draw on their own strengths and resources and reach a resolution of their inner pain. It is humbling to see what simple acts of courtesy can do and distressing to realize how often these are omitted. Nevertheless, it is with patients who make us feel most inadequate that from time to time come moments of clarity that seem given from outside. Some would call it grace; others do not use this word but can still recognize that a bridge has somehow been built toward a place of unexpected resolution.

Our busy and increasingly materialistic world has cut many

of us off from the deep wisdom that is still to be seen in those with a well-tried faith and others with a spirituality quite outside any specifically religious content. The hospice and palliative care movement constantly refers to its commitment not only to physical and psychosocial problems, but also to the need for spiritual help, often without making any attempt at definition. Michael Kearney here introduces us to a pain that comes from the depths of a person's being. Not all of us will have the knowledge and ability to work with the skills described in the fascinating stories that follow, but enlightened awareness of this neglected area will help to balance the contemporary lack of interest in the things of the spirit. Waiting alongside a patient in silence or meeting practical needs are never to be disparaged or avoided, and many patients will find in these all they need to give them assurance and peace.

We should not be too daunted by this challenge. The way care is given can reach the most hidden places and give space for unexpected development. We frequently see how both patient and family may find peace and strength for themselves when we know we have given so little. There are possibilities in people facing death that are a constant astonishment. We will see them more often if we can gain the confidence to approach our fellows without hiding behind a professional mask, instead meeting as one person to another, both aware of the depths of a pain that somehow has its healing within itself. In this discovery we may find out as much about living as about dying. People at the end of their lives will then be our teachers.

CICELY SAUNDERS, OM, DBE, FRCP,
Chairman, St. Christopher's Hospice, London,
May 1995

Introduction

To fear death is neither a sign of weakness nor a reason for shame. Like our ability to feel joy and pain, it is part of what it means to be alive and human. For most of us the focus of this fear is the actual dying process itself, what it is going to be like as we are going through it, rather than what might, or might not, happen afterward. We may fear the anticipated physical pain and distress, the emotional pain of separation from those we love, and the dependency and loss of control which we imagine lie ahead. Furthermore, for many of us these fears are compounded by the experience of having had someone we care about die badly, perhaps in great pain or unsupported and alone.

In addition to these specific and personal fears, there are other deeper layers to our fear of dying and death. We all share that primal, instinctive fear of the dark which Bacon speaks of, and I believe that it is this existential and primal fear of the unknown that can generate that particular form of human suffering I call "soul pain." In psychological terms, the prime mover in this is that aspect of the human mind known as the "ego," which is happiest when in control of a familiar and predictable world but which is profoundly threatened by the approach of death, which it sees as utter chaos and the ultimate unknown. In a frantic attempt to survive, the ego may project its fear of death onto the deep and unconscious aspects of mind, the "soul," seeing in its unfamiliar and unpredictable depths a microcosm

15

of death itself. In a reaction aimed at ensuring its survival, our panicking ego then flees from soul, thereby alienating itself from all that is deepest in us and leaving us feeling isolated and terrified in a wasteland of meaninglessness and hopelessness— soul pain.

There is, in addition, a cultural level to the fear that surfaces as we approach death. What we see in the frightened eyes of a dying person may well be more than an individual response overlaying a shared and basic human survival reaction. Our terror of death also reflects the deep split that has occurred in the West between the rational and the intuitive aspects of mind. As, down through the centuries, we in the West have increasingly prized the mind's ability to reason and to understand, we have simultaneously ignored, forgotten, or devalued its potential to imagine, to wonder, and to know intuitively, all of which are aspects of soul. Evidence of this split is abundant and is illustrated by historical and contemporary examples. While the industrial and scientific revolutions might be seen as among its more positive consequences, Hiroshima, Auschwitz, and the devastation of the planet are testament to its escalating negative effect. I believe that a dying individual's suffering may also be a personal expression of this bigger cultural disconnection from soul.

If one allows that this may be even partially true, it is hardly surprising that some people have an inordinately difficult time in their dying and that caregivers occasionally encounter patients whom it seems impossible to comfort. To believe that it is possible to sort out this cultural problem, by "making it all better" in the individual arena, indicates a deluded sense of our own omnipotence and a dangerous naïveté that can lead to an inexorable downward spiral of repeated failure, burnout, and despair.

I do not say this to rationalize the sense of inadequacy we may experience when confronted with soul pain in someone close to death—although it may help us understand why we can feel this way—but to make the point that what we choose to do in response to soul pain matters. If we do nothing, we are colluding with and compounding this damaging cultural malaise. In the short term this may seem like a successful ploy in that it can keep our angst at bay. The danger with this ploy is that it is as shortsighted as it will be short lasting, and this has implications for each one of us. By not addressing these issues now we may be creating an impossible task for ourselves in the future. As long as this personal and cultural splitting off from soul persists, fear and meaninglessness will continue to dominate the final days of vulnerable individuals. In contrast, and as many stories in this book illustrate, if we can find a creative way of responding to the challenge of soul pain it may open up a path to the very heart of living, even in the shadow of death.

How and where might we begin this process? My experience of working as a doctor within the hospice movement has shown me just what an impact the combined approach of multiprofessional expertise and compassionate attention to the whole person can make. We can make the process of dying easier by expertly controlling an individual's pain and other physical symptoms, while fostering open and honest communication with them and their families. This can transform what may have been a frightening and miserable existence into a time of continuing personal growth and of completion.

The hospice movement, which has done so much to allay the specific fears and distress associated with the dying process, has origins which can be traced back to the caring impulse at the root of all health professions. It has evolved in this century as a redress to the imbalance created by an increasingly scientific and technological medical system. In the past twenty-five years the principles of treatment and care which were developed within this movement have begun to be integrated into mainstream western medicine and have led to the international dissemination of this new, yet old, health care specialty now known as "palliative care."

However, while the stories I share in this book show that what pioneer hospice worker Cicely Saunders calls this "effective loving care" of the dying is essential, they also reveal that sometimes more is necessary in responding to soul pain. Albert Kreinheder, writing from his own experience of living with terminal illness, offers a clue as to what this something "more" might be when he writes: "It doesn't matter when you die so much as how you die. Not by what means, but whether or not you are altogether in one piece, psychologically speaking." This suggests that a quest for inner wholeness, understood more in terms of commitment to a process than achievement of a goal, might inform the direction of our response. And if the theory is correct that the root of this problem is a personal and cultural disconnection from and a devaluing of all that is soul, then the initial direction we must take in this quest is inward and, as archetypal psychologist James Hillman emphasizes in his writings, *downward.*

There is another dimension to this discussion which I want to emphasize at this stage. The stories throughout this book repeatedly and consistently endorse the comments of Jungian analyst and writer Marie Louise von Franz that "Nature, through dreams, prepares us for death." To focus on soul pain purely in terms of what *we* can, or cannot, do about it, may mean that we fail to recognize the extraordinary role which I believe the soul itself plays in the healing process. The deep psyche is more than a passive dustbin for our unwanted thoughts, memories, and emotions. It also contains autonomous elements which are concerned with psychological wholeness, and it is my experience that this process of deep inner healing becomes accelerated in the dying. It is as though this bottomless pool, so despised by the terrified ego, not only contains a healing balm in its black depths but is waiting with longing to apply this to our mortal wound, if only we allow it to do so. If the dying person even begins to attend to soul, soul responds a thousandfold.

In this book I explore the nature of soul pain in those close to death. I do this by sharing and reflecting on the stories of a number of individuals with far advanced illness in the light of two models, one mythological and the other psychological. Some of these stories illustrate a particular way of working with the deep inner aspects of a dying person's experience and show that this work is essentially a cooperative venture with the healing forces of the person's own psyche. This inner or depth work is the essential complement to the outer care of the individual and may enable that person to find his or her own way through the prison of soul pain to a place of greater wholeness, a new depth of living, and a falling away of fear.

PART 1

STORIES AND QUESTIONS

It's possible I am pushing through solid rock
in flintlike layers, as the ore lies, alone;
I am such a long way in I see no way through,
and no space: everything is close to my face,
and everything close to my face is stone.

I don't have much knowledge yet in grief—
so this massive darkness makes me feel small.
You be the master: make yourself fierce, break in:
then your great transforming will happen to me,
and my great grief cry will happen to you.

RAINER MARIA RILKE
(translated by Robert Bly)

I have seen many people die. There may have been pain, but this was eased by the skill of their caregivers. There may have been great sadness, anger, or fear, but these feelings no longer overwhelmed when they were shared with another who was prepared to listen. Although some of these individuals never spoke of death, there was nearly always the sense that they nonetheless "knew." In some detail each person marked their dying as uniquely their own, and when death eventually came, there was often a sense of waiting and of readiness. Even if the dying had been a struggle, death itself seemed to bring with it a natural ease, a peacefulness, and the sort of relief one feels as a friend takes from one's back a heavy load.

However, no matter how skilled or humane our care of the dying is, it does not, and cannot, "make it all better." As one person, whose story I tell in a later chapter, said to me just hours before her death, "It's not all right." No matter what we might do to make it easier, death remains the ultimate separation, the ultimate unknown. And there are some who, as poet Dylan Thomas puts it, "Do not go gentle into that good night." These include those whose dying has become a time of terrified struggle or meaninglessness despite the best efforts of family and caregivers to comfort and palliate their distress. It is individuals such as these who have been my greatest teachers. In their suffering they have challenged me to go a step further, to search for another way, and to turn, with them, toward the unknown.

> It is too late to start
> For destinations not of the heart
> I must stay here with my hurt.
> R. S. THOMAS, from "Here"

Jackie

Jackie was in her early fifties, a music teacher in a girls' school, described by a friend as someone who was always "bright, brusque, and breezy." Her family doctor had referred her to the hospice for control of a long-standing and severe pain in her right leg. Two years previously she had had a hysterectomy because of cancer and had subsequently remained well until the pain had started. A scan showed that the tumor had recurred and was invading the muscles and nerves on the back wall of her abdomen. Despite treatment with radiotherapy and painkillers, both the tumor and the pain had worsened.

By the time Jackie was admitted to the hospice, she was confined to bed because of pain. The nurses caring for her described her as a woman who was terrified of even the slightest movement in case it should worsen her pain. When I asked her how she saw her situation at that time, she replied, "I honestly believe it's all due to a fall I had from my bike last September." I felt that she was denying the seriousness of her situation and that this was probably contributing to her difficulties. This was confirmed when her close friend, Jean, spoke of how she had confronted Jackie some weeks previously with the fact that the cancer had recurred. Apparently, while this had initially triggered an outburst of tears, Jackie had then been much better for days afterward.

Even though it became increasingly evident to all caring for Jackie that her pain was due as much to her fear and denial as to the cancer invading the nerves of her leg, she herself was adamant that it was simply a mechanical and physical problem. Looking me straight in the eye she would ask, "And what are you going to do about it?" Over the next two weeks we tried a variety of usually successful medications. Simultaneously, different members of the ward team attempted to approach the psychological aspects of her pain both directly (by asking her how she was feeling and whether or not she had any questions or worries) and indirectly (through massage). However, all these efforts were to no avail. Her pain worsened and was now exacerbated by a rising sense of disappointment and desperation, feelings which I and other members of the team were also beginning to experience.

At around this time I met Jean again. We discussed Jackie's situation and decided that we should meet her the following morning. We could see no way forward other than to confront her, as gently as possible, with the hard truth of her situation. Although we had serious reservations about this plan, our hypothesis was that her denial was no longer working as a helpful psychological defense but rather was exacerbating her distress by isolating her in a prison of fear which, in turn, was making her pain worse.

That afternoon, before any such confrontation, Jackie's defenses cracked in an eruption of uncontrollable fear, paranoia, and pain. She writhed about in her bed as she groaned, hyperventilated, and cried out, wide-eyed, for someone to help. When the nurses came, she became even more terrified, accusing them of trying to kill her and refusing their offers of additional pain and tranquilizing medication. When, with her friend's persuasion, she eventually agreed to take the medication, it appeared to have little or no effect. Jackie's panic and agitation worsened, as did our sense of utter impotence.

Jean and the nurses stayed with Jackie throughout that evening. They held her in their arms and spoke soothingly in an attempt to calm and comfort her, but to no avail. Eventually we took a decision to give her medication to sedate her. She soon drifted off into a fitful and uneasy sleep.

Jackie was still sedated and sleeping deeply when I visited her the following morning. I called her name, and her eyes flickered open in momentary panic but then shut again. I asked her how she was. In words that were slurred and barely audible she replied that she was "climbing in the mountains with Jean."

Over the next few days we tried, on a number of occasions, to lighten the sedation. However, each time Jackie began to waken she was terrified and cried out, and although we sat and held her she remained agitated and would not settle until we had given her further sedative medication. The nurses and I met her family and Jean. We agreed that the only way we could treat this anguish and pain was to keep her asleep. Over the following weekend Jackie developed pneumonia and died.

While my training in palliative care had introduced me to a holistic model of pain which acknowledged that the "total pain" of the dying individual was a multifaceted and dynamic experience with social, emotional, and spiritual as well as physical dimensions, I still felt utterly ill equipped to deal with Jackie's overwhelming fear and suffering. I simply did not have the means to describe, let alone respond to, what was happening in her situation.

Jackie left me with feelings of disappointment and failure and a number of unanswered questions. When confronted with anguish like hers, did I have to accept that there was nothing I, nor indeed anyone else, could do to make it better? When I attempted to help someone like Jackie, whose pain was I ultimately trying to alleviate, mine or hers? And what precisely was the nature of this particular form of suffering? I felt sure that if I had a better understanding of this it would point me toward another way, a more appropriate way, of responding to someone in such distress.

Emma's and Bill's Stories

Emma was in her sixties and had terminal cancer of the ovary. She was a committed evangelical Christian who had spent most of her life working as a lay missionary in Africa. Even though she knew just how ill she was, she did not accept that this meant that she was going to die.

Emma suffered from a constant feeling of nausea which proved resistant to all our therapeutic efforts. In addition she was troubled, restless, and unhappy in herself. At each visit she greeted me by saying she was "No better—but don't worry, God is just testing my faith. I *know* He is going to cure me."

As the weeks went by, Emma became increasingly distressed. She was by then very much weaker, while the miracle she had been expecting had not happened. Then, one day, I knew as I sat by her bedside that something had changed. She told me that since she had woken up that day she had felt different in herself. She said that the sickening feeling in the pit of her stomach had gone, and she appeared calm and relaxed. We talked for a while, and as I went to leave, she took my hand and looking in my eyes said, "I know that I am being healed." Emma remained comfortable and at peace in herself until she died a few days later.

Bill, a fifty-nine-year-old agnostic with terminal lung cancer, had just a few weeks to live. His heavy drinking down through the years had resulted in his losing his job and becoming estranged from his family. While at home, he had been assessed by the hospice home care team. The nurse who made the initial home visit found a man who was so short of breath that he was unable to say more than three or four words at a time. He looked terrified and told her that he did not want to hear any-

28

thing about his illness unless it was "good news." On advice from the home care team, Bill's family doctor had then prescribed some medication to try to ease his breathlessness, but this had little beneficial effect. As he was daily becoming more fearful and anxious and had no one to care for him at home, he was offered a bed in the hospice. He immediately accepted this.

Within a couple of days of admission, Bill appeared more relaxed and comfortable. We wondered why his medication, which had remained unchanged since his admission, should suddenly have taken effect but felt this was probably due to a greater sense of security in his new surroundings.

One day, in the course of doing a ward round, I stopped by Bill's bedside. "How are you today, Bill?" I asked, expecting him to speak of his breathlessness or his bowels or some other "safe" topic. Instead, his reply left me stunned. "It's hard to describe," he began, ". . . contentment, happiness, it's something that's come on gradually these last five weeks, not at any one particular moment. And I was awful before—so breathless and scared. I thought I would choke to death. Things had been swirling around outside and inside too, like the snow in one of those Christmas toys, but it slowly and eventually settled as . . . truth, yes, that sums it up—TRUTH. It's an experience, something inside myself, comes from here [pointing at the center of his chest]. I feel proud of myself to think I have it in me. It's not that I'm religious. While I respect all that stuff, it doesn't seem to be about that for me now." As he finished we sat in silence together for a while. I then asked him if he had any sense of what would happen when he died. "I don't know," he said, "I've never done it before! I sometimes think, 'Nobody will want you, Bill.' I don't know. I believe it's about living, not dying. If there is something afterwards, that's okay, too. No, I'm not afraid of dying." Bill died, very peacefully, a week after this conversation.

Emma's and Bill's arrivals in a place of inner healing and fearlessness contrasted starkly with Jackie's unresolved anguish.

But what precisely had brought about such radical transformation in these two very different people? I remember thinking that if I could even begin to understand this, it might be hugely relevant for someone like Jackie. The only thing that was clear to me at the time, however, was that whatever had happened for Emma and for Bill was because of some subtle yet powerful change within the individuals themselves. I wondered if this seemingly spontaneous and haphazard process was, in its very essence, beyond comprehension.

Sean

Sean was in his early thirties and had been living and working as a teacher in France. Three years previously he had noticed a lump in his right leg. Since it was painful and getting bigger by the day he decided to go to see a doctor. Hospital admission and investigation revealed a malignant tumor of his right sciatic nerve. Following major surgery to his leg he made a full recovery and was soon back at work again. Two years later he noticed another painful swelling, this time on the right side of his chest. This was diagnosed as a secondary tumor. He had another operation and was started on chemotherapy. The following January he returned to Ireland for a second opinion. The oncologist started him on a further course of chemotherapy.

By March, Sean had severe pain in his chest and was losing weight. This suggested that, despite this treatment, the cancer was progressing. His general practitioner referred him as an outpatient to the hospice, for pain control. It was at this stage that Sean and I first met. I remember noticing, as he came through the door, that he was in obvious pain. He spoke of his cancer openly and said he felt sure the new course of chemotherapy would be a success. When I asked about his family, he told me that his father had died when he was in his teens and that he was staying at his mother's home while in Dublin and seeing a lot of his four sisters, who lived nearby. He added that this was only a temporary arrangement, because he was planning to return to France again before too long.

Sean then described the severe and constant pain he had in the right side of his chest, which was only partially eased by the medication he was on at that time. As I examined him, I found that he was very sore and hypersensitive to even the lightest touch in that area. I made a clinical diagnosis of pain caused by tumor invading the muscle, bone, and nerves of his right rib cage. He was by then already on a high dose of morphine for the pain. I asked him to increase the dose of morphine and started him on some additional medication which I hoped would help.

In early April, I saw Sean again in the outpatient clinic. He told me that his pain was no better. After discussion, I arranged his admission to the hospital so that he could have local anesthetic injected into the nerves of his chest to try to numb the pain. Once again this was to no avail. In mid-April, he returned to France for two weeks. Immediately after his return to Ireland, his general practitioner telephoned the hospice asking if he could be urgently admitted. She described him as being "in desperate agony."

When he arrived at the hospice Sean was pale, clammy, agitated, and obviously in very severe pain. I thought that the mechanism of his pain was the same as before, although he was now obviously extremely frightened. Over the next few days I made some changes in his medication, including a further increase in his morphine and the addition of a strong tranquilizer. I arranged for the anesthetist to see him again, and he performed another procedure to try to numb the pain, this time by inserting a small tube through the right side of his chest which we could use to administer a constant infusion of local anesthetic.

Unfortunately, none of these interventions seemed to give any lasting benefit, and by the end of his second week in the hospice Sean was saying that his pain was "the worst it had ever been." The nurses' records from this time suggest that he felt the situation was out of control, with words such as "desperate" and "panic" being used to describe his distress.

At a team meeting called to discuss Sean's situation, we noted that his nights were bad because of overwhelming pain when he was awake and frightening nightmares when he managed to sleep. In addition, some of the nursing staff reported inconsistent and inexplicable responses to medication given for breakthrough pain. Finally, different members of the ward team spoke of how Sean was prepared to talk of his now obviously very advanced illness only in terms of it being a "temporary setback" and of how he was "utterly convinced that the chemotherapy was going to work."

Despite general agreement that there was an active emotional component to Sean's pain, a number of staff shared similar stories of attempting to approach him at this level and their feelings of frustration at repeatedly failing to reach him. As we discussed what else we could possibly do to help, our options appeared limited. We could either persist with our current approach in the hope that time and perseverance might bring a change, or we could further increase his sedative medication. Even though we had a sense of having gone close to the limit of what we could offer, we agreed to persist with the current line of treatment and to review progress in a week's time.

It was at this point of desperation that I first considered the possibility of doing some imagework with Sean. I had trained in this way of working with imagery and felt that this approach might give him the access to his unconscious mind which he needed if he was to make contact with and express the deep, hidden emotion which I believed lay buried there. If this was successful, I felt sure it would lead to a lessening of his physical pain.

I visited Sean later that day and, sitting by his bedside, attempted to explain to him how this technique, which I described as a type of visualization, might possibly help him. I first spoke to him about the nature of pain and said that it was something which affected not just a person's body but also their mind, feelings, and spirit, which is why we referred to it as "total pain." I then drew a triangular iceberg, with its tip showing above the surface. Below the surface lay the enormous bulk of the iceberg.

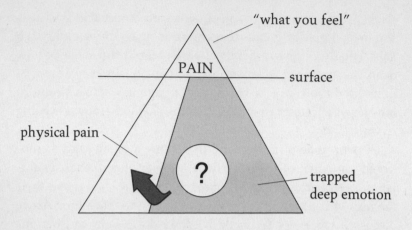

"This," I said, pointing at the iceberg, "is like your pain. What you feel is like the tip here, above the surface. But, as with this iceberg, the roots of your pain lie deep beneath the surface. Some of these we know about, for example the physical basis of your pain, and this has been valuable in directing the treatment. However, your pain has not responded as we had hoped and expected, and there *may* be other aspects to it, such as emotions which are trapped so deep down there that even you are unaware of them. If these deep emotions are unrecognized, perhaps their only way out is through the physical pain, which could be the reason your pain has been so difficult to control. Imagework may allow this buried emotion to find its own expression through imagery, so that it no longer has to use your physical pain as its megaphone."

"If it's going to help my pain," he replied, "I'm willing to give it a try. *Anything . . .*"

I then told him in detail what was involved in this way of working; that it would mean our setting aside an hour or so of uninterrupted time, that for the most part it would consist of him sitting there with his eyes closed, attending to what was happening in the "mind's eye" of his imagination, and that my role would be to give him instructions, make suggestions, or ask him questions. I emphasized that if at any stage he felt anxious or uncomfortable with what was going on, he was completely at liberty to open his eyes, and we could discuss what was happening.

We held the first imagework session in a quiet room off the ward the following afternoon. Sean looked pale, uncomfortable, and ill and decided at the beginning to lie on the couch. After a simple introductory relaxation exercise, I led him through a guided visualization. In this I invited him to imagine himself in a small rowboat on a flat, calm sea. As he rowed he could feel the warm sun on his face and the gentle wind in his hair. After he had rowed for a while, I invited him to put the oars on the floor of the boat and, if he chose to do so, to slowly and carefully get over the side and lower himself into the water. For a short time he remained like this, holding on to the side of the boat, aware of the sensation of warm water enveloping his body. I then invited him, should he so wish, to imagine himself letting go of the boat, noting how he felt as he did this, and to tell me what happened then. He described how he decided to let go and found himself floating and how he began to splash and play as he swam through the water. He said that he looked up then and saw that, without his noticing, the boat had drifted to quite a distance away and that he began to panic and was frightened that he was going to drown. At this point, I suggested that the boat had come nearer to him, and he found he was able to get in, back to safety.

Every step in this process involved a choice on Sean's part, and he was free to stop at any point. Toward the end of this visualization I asked him to pull back in his imagination and to observe himself in the boat. I then asked the question, "As you look at Sean in this situation can you tell me what you see and what it is you feel Sean most wants and needs right now?" Without hesitating he answered, "He's kneeling, face down and exhausted on the floor of the boat. He needs reassurance." He began to cry and continued to weep for some time as he spoke of his father, who had died fifteen years previously. He said how much he was missing him and that he felt his father's presence would have given him the reassurance he needed. The session ended with my acknowledging the courage required to do what he had just done and our agreeing to meet and work in this way again.

Over the following week Sean's ward notes reported a definite improvement in his pain. We were able to remove the local anesthetic tube and to reduce the dose of both the morphine and tranquilizer because, unlike previously, they were now making him excessively drowsy. He was sleeping well, and what occasional pain he had responded consistently when he was given an additional dose of painkiller.

In addition to the obvious physical improvement in his condition, however, staff members began to talk about a change which they noticed in Sean himself—a definite yet very subtle change. He was still Sean, but he was no longer the desperate, struggling prisoner he had been. While previously his pain had dominated his every waking moment and been the only thing he wanted to discuss with staff, he now had a very different attitude to what pain he still had. For instance, he would say, "The pain is still there at times, but I can live with it now. It's no longer the problem it was before." He appeared more relaxed, more able to sink back into his pillows, as he chatted about his life in France and, in contrast to previously, he now seemed to want to get to know the people caring for him.

On May 25 Sean was discharged to the care of his mother and sisters and his family doctor, with a plan for the hospice home care team also to become involved. As he and I had grown close during his time in the hospice, and as he felt the imagework we had done together had been helpful, we agreed to continue to work together in this way at approximately fortnightly intervals.

In the weeks following his discharge, Sean remained virtu-

ally free of pain, although it was evident to all that he was growing steadily thinner and weaker. During that time, when he was
still fairly mobile, one of his family would drive him in to the
hospice so that we could meet. Such meetings would begin with
a brief chat about how he was feeling, physically and emotionally, and we would deal at this stage with any changes that were
needed in his medical treatment. For the most part his symptoms were minor and not a source of great anxiety. We both
knew that the real purpose of these meetings was what we came
to call "the image check-in." This occasionally meant talking
about any dreams he had had since we previously met that had
stayed with him or that seemed particularly powerful or relevant. Usually, however, the check-in consisted in my inviting
him to close his eyes, to relax, and to ask his imagination for an
image of anything he needed to look at on that particular day.
The following description is of an imagework session which is
typical of those held during his final weeks. It occurred when he
came to see me in the outpatient clinic of the hospice on June 5.

Sean had arrived that day looking pale and complaining of
feeling dizzy and nauseated. After a short time discussing the
events of recent days, I led him through the by now familiar
relaxation exercise. At this stage I invited him to bring his
attention to the sensation of nausea and asked him to allow an
image to come into his mind which would describe this experience, an image which might show him something he needed to
become aware of. Immediately he replied that he was standing
in a little boat, looking at an enormous liner which was slowly
beginning to pull out of the harbor. He felt he would really like
to be on the bigger boat. I asked him to imagine himself on the
deck of the liner and to describe what he saw. He spoke of how,
when he looked over the rails of the liner, he could see the small
boat he had been in and of his surprise at noticing that there was
in fact another person in it now, an old man who looked like a
sea captain. He began to dialogue with this man, saying that he

felt admiration for him and that he realized that "someone needed to stay to look after the harbor." The old man replied, "We each have our own way." When I asked him what he felt as he began this journey, Sean replied, "I feel a bit anxious, since I don't know where this boat is going, and when I look back at the harbor wall and see those I love standing there, I feel sad. But I also feel excitement, light, sun, life. I sense I will see beautiful things along the way. I love traveling."

In subsequent sessions, images of boats of different shapes and sizes recurred as part of a theme of going on a journey. The feelings expressed in these sessions ranged from disappointment, anxiety, fear, and sadness to enjoyment, excitement, and hope. Throughout this time those of us caring for Sean agreed that, despite his now obviously weakening condition, he remained surprisingly "well in himself."

During what turned out to be our final imagework session, held in his own home on July 12, two weeks before he died, Sean found himself wandering through a foggy landscape. I invited him to imagine himself coming upon a treasure chest which he could open if he wanted to, and which would contain something he really needed at that time. He lifted the lid, looked inside, and found a "wonderful sleek white speedboat. It's got no engine. It doesn't need one. It runs on air." He said he felt this boat could bring him "through the fog to where it was clear."

He got in the boat and it did indeed carry him out of the fog. There he saw a young man of about seventeen with a blood-stained white shirt. He was bleeding from his wounded chest. The young man was not alone. There was a young woman with him of about the same age. He was bent forward; she was supporting him with her arm around him. At first she did not appreciate how badly injured he was, but then she saw his wound and led him toward the hospital.

During those final weeks and days, Sean never once openly discussed his deterioration or poor prognosis with me or any other member of the hospice team, although he no longer spoke of expecting to be cured. Some weeks after his death, I received a letter from his mother, thanking me and all who had cared for Sean. She ended by saying, "The fact that you talked to Sean allowed him to talk to us about his death shortly before he died. We think that gave him peace, and it was a great help to us."

Sean was a teacher and I, for one, learned a lot from him. After his death I felt a mixture of sadness and relief. I was also surprised that things had worked out for him as well as they had and puzzled as to how this had happened. Prior to the image-work, Sean's escalating distress was reminiscent of Jackie's, as was my own sense of impotence and rising panic. His agony had been a mixture of horrendous physical pain and fear of what this pain signified. Our counseling efforts as a team of care-givers had come to nothing because of his refusal to see his pain other than as a purely physical problem. Certainly the first imagework session appeared to be a turning point for Sean. But why was this so?

I had learned about imagework as part of a training in psy-chotherapy, and had personally experienced it as a powerful psychological technique. I was also aware of recent work done with visualization in a variety of medical conditions and knew that it had been shown to lead to physiological changes through the mediation of the nonvoluntary or autonomic nervous sys-tem. My deciding to offer Sean the opportunity to work in this way had been purely in the hope that it might help his physical pain. I can now see that this psychotherapeutic move was more a naive and desperate grasping at straws than part of some care-fully planned strategy. My motivations were, at best, mixed, and doing imagework with someone in such emotional despera-tion was not without risk. Yes, of course I had wanted to help Sean and relieve his awful physical pain, but I was also doing something because I found it too hard to do nothing, and because I was unhappy with the suggestion, at that time favored by a minority of the ward team, that we should give him more sedation.

While I was delighted that this intervention seemed to bring a real improvement in Sean's physical pain, what amazed and confused me was the subtle but definite psychological change which also became apparent in Sean and which was commented on by his family as well as by those caring for him. Whereas in the recent past I had found it extremely uncomfortable to sit with him, it was now a pleasure. I came away from such meetings feeling that in some way I was the one who was being reassured and comforted.

Once again I was left wondering, as I had with Emma and with Bill in the past, what precisely had occurred. Now, however, I seemed to have a signpost: the change had occurred following Sean's entry into the world of his imagination. Somehow, this encounter with the images that arose from his deepest inner experience had radically, if quietly, transformed the quality of his living and his dying.

PART 2

SIGNS AND SYMPTOMS

This clumsy living that moves lumbering
as if in ropes through what is not done
reminds us of the awkward way the swan walks.

And to die, which is a letting go
of the ground we stand on and cling to every day,
is like the swan when he nervously lets himself down

into the water, which receives him gaily
and which flows under
and after him, wave after wave,
while the swan, unmoving and marvelously calm,
is pleased to be carried, each minute more fully grown,
more like a king, composed, farther and farther on.

RAINER MARIA RILKE, "The Swan"
(translated by Robert Bly)

Encountering suffering like Jackie's, and its occasional and seemingly inexplicable resolution in individuals like Emma, Bill, and Sean, confronted me with questions to which I had no answers. These unanswered questions have motivated in me a personal and professional quest over many years. During this time I have found two models, one mythological and the other psychological, and a particular vocabulary and terminology that seem to offer a helpful way of looking at, naming, and responding to such suffering.

We might say that at this moment, as in the time of Galileo, what we most urgently need is much less new facts (there are enough and even embarrassingly more than enough of these in every quarter) than a new way of looking at the facts and accepting them. A new way of seeing, combined with a new way of acting—that is what we need.

TEILHARD DE CHARDIN

Chiron:
A Mythological Model

The Greek myth of Chiron, the wounded healer, is an ancient version of the desperate struggle I had witnessed in Jackie and in Sean. It offers a mythological way of understanding both the nature of such distress and how an individual might begin to move beyond such suffering to a place of healing.

Although this myth was probably first told about three thousand years ago, at the dawn of Western civilization, its origins are thought to be far more ancient, going back over one hundred thousand years to the universal shamanic stories of Paleolithic times. These stories told of tribal priest-physicians, the original wounded healers, whose ability to heal others was seen as being directly linked to their having journeyed in depth into their own wounded selves.

What seems particularly relevant about the Chiron myth is that, as the first Western telling of the universal story of the wounded healer, it appears to embody the archeological foundations of many of our contemporary attitudes to suffering and death in a form that is especially tailored for Western consciousness. It offers a new (yet very old) way of looking at and working with the particular type of suffering which I had witnessed in individuals like Jackie and Sean, and it speaks clearly and powerfully to me in my own experience.

Chiron was born a centaur, with a human head and torso and the body of a horse, because he was conceived when his father, one of the gods, disguised in the form of a horse, raped a mortal nymph. He was, consequently, both half horse, half human and half mortal, half immortal. Abandoned and rejected at birth, he was adopted by the sun-god Apollo, who reared him and taught him all he knew. Chiron became a wise and respected teacher, renowned for his shrewd intelligence and many skills. He was mentor to some of Greece's greatest heroes, including Hercules.

Although Chiron was civilized and cultured, this could not be said for other centaurs, who were renowned for their tendency to go berserk after drinking wine. One day, at a wedding banquet, fighting broke out between an unruly group of drunk centaurs and the rest of the guests. Hercules, who was among the guests, fired a poisoned arrow at the centaurs to quell their rioting. Chiron happened to be standing in their midst, and the arrow struck him in the knee. As Chiron was half immortal, the poisoned arrow did not kill him but instead inflicted an agonizing and unhealable wound.

If the first half of Chiron's life had brought him success and acclaim among the kings and heroes of Greece, the next part saw him becoming a recluse, as he withdrew to his mountainside to tend his wound and begin a desperate search for release from his suffering. This search was to last the rest of his life. While he could not find his own cure, he became wise in the use of all forms of healing herbs and compassionate to the suffering of others. Those who now visited him were not the rich and powerful but the blind and the lame and those in pain, and he welcomed them and brought them comfort. They called him "the wounded healer" and wondered why he could not heal himself.

One day Hercules returned, bringing news that if Chiron was willing to sacrifice his immortality on behalf of Prometheus, who was being punished for mocking the Gods, he too could be freed of his suffering. Chiron agreed to this; he died and descended to the underworld. For nine days and nine nights he remained in the darkness of death. Then Zeus, recognizing the generosity of this sacrifice, took pity on Chiron and restored his immortality, raising him to the heavens as a constellation of stars.

Chiron's behavior in this myth is determined by two radically different viewpoints. The first of these, which I call "the heroic stance," is evident in the successes and struggles of the early part of the story. The pivotal moment where this viewpoint shifts to the other comes as Chiron chooses to let go of his immortality as he swaps places with Prometheus. From here his actions come from a new viewpoint, "the way of descent." This turnabout marks a transition from one realm to another, from the above to the below, from the known to the unknown.

THE HEROIC STANCE AND THE MEDICAL MODEL

Chiron's early life, first as conscientious pupil of his stepfather and mentor, Apollo, and later as teacher of the sons of Grecian kings, shows that he was closely identified with the heroic stance. This is the same heroic attitude that underpins scientific Western health care, where it is referred to as the "medical model."

The medical model states that (all) illnesses of body and mind have (if one looks hard enough) an underlying cause; if one can find this cause (diagnosis) and proceed to remove, reverse, replace, or bypass it (treatment), one can return to the status quo (cure). It is evident that, as models go, the medical model works well. It has led to cures being found for an ever-increasing number of illnesses. It has resulted in an extension in quantity of life and an improvement in quality of life for countless sick individuals.

Where the medical model and the heroic stance which informs it run into trouble is in confrontation with insoluble problems. In the Chiron myth this happens when Chiron is wounded by a poisoned arrow from the bow of one of his prize pupils—ironically the very embodiment of the heroic principle, Hercules. The resulting wound is not only agonizing but incurable. The analogous situation in Western health care is when a patient's illness is diagnosed as terminal. For each of us such a moment inevitably comes. No matter how it occurs, and whatever unique way we have of dealing with it, we will all one day discover that, like Chiron, we too are mortally wounded.

Chiron's immediate and continuing reaction to his wounding is mirrored time and time again in our reactions both as patients and health care professionals. When the initial shock wears off, the unrelenting search for a remedy and the struggle to get out of this prison of suffering begins. The attitudes which inform the heroic stance run deep, and for each of us they will usually have been repeatedly validated by our overcoming previous life crises. We suppose that it is simply a matter of trying ever harder or of looking ever farther afield for that elusive cure, but this response engenders an emotional pain that is characterized by feelings of frustration and powerlessness and a growing fear of what the future might hold. These feelings are compounded by hurt pride and an indignant sense of disbelief that a way out, a cure, cannot be found despite all one's courage, ingenuity, and best efforts.

PARADIGM SHIFT TO THE WAY OF DESCENT

What then—to die exhausted like a trapped bird against a windowpane?

The story of Chiron suggests that there may be another way, the way identified by Hercules when he told Chiron of the opportunity to exchange places with Prometheus. The path he pointed toward was neither up nor across but led downward, into the very center of Chiron's wound and the source of his darkest fears. This was the way of descent.

The radical turnabout at the center of the Chiron myth is an example of what is called a "paradigm shift." A paradigm is a mental frame of reference or way of viewing a situation. Every time we look at and then respond to a given set of circumstances, we do so in the context of a particular paradigm. We may see and respond to exactly the same situation in a variety of ways depending on what paradigm we are operating from at any given moment. For most of us our only awareness of paradigms comes in the immediate aftermath of moving from one paradigm to another, when we may temporarily be aware that a familiar reality is being viewed and responded to in a new way. An example of this is the little boy who was terrified each night by the monster snoring in the wall next to his bed. When his parents took him next door and showed him the gurgling bath pipe, the little boy saw the situation completely differently and was no longer afraid of the noises. A paradigm shift had occurred.

The heroic stance represents one paradigm, the way of descent another. From the perspective of the heroic stance Chiron's mortal wound is seen as a problem to be solved and an obstacle to getting on with life as it used to be. From the perspective of the way of descent, it becomes the way through his suffering to a new order of reality, a gateway to healing. This profound change in perspective costs Chiron, as poet T. S. Eliot puts it, "not less than everything" and is made possible by a combination of factors, including correct timing, external agents and events, and individual choice.

Both these paradigms are essential at different times and in very different ways in the process of dying. The heroic stance is usually the dominant paradigm at the earlier stages of the terminal illness and is apparent in efforts made to alleviate and contain the physical, emotional, and social aspects of the individual's suffering. It is also possible that the wounding is not in fact a mortal wounding and that there is still a way out to be found, if only one struggles hard and long enough to find it. Furthermore, this paradigm has value beyond its immediate effects, in that it helps to create the emotional conditions that facilitate the essential paradigm shift. A time comes for all who are dying when they know that they and those around them have done all that it is possible to do, when they realize that the heroic stance has achieved all it can and where a continued struggle against the inevitable is not only futile but damaging and is adding to their pain and suffering. When, at this moment, such individuals let go of their struggle and let themselves go with the pull of inner gravity, the new paradigm, the way of descent, has already begun.

For people who suffer, a move into the way of descent represents a radical change in perspective. Even though their circumstances may remain exactly the same, they will now experience them in a very different way. It is as if they have moved from a cramped place where fear was dominant to a more open space. A lessening of emotional pressure and feelings of sadness and the reemergence of a sense of meaning are some signs that this shift has occurred.

THE FIVE PARTS OF THE CHIRON MYTH

While "the heroic stance" and "the way of descent" describe the two underlying paradigms in the Chiron myth, its value as a tool for understanding the experience of dying individuals is enhanced when looked at in terms of the five discrete parts that form the whole. These are: the wounding, the struggle, the choice, the descent, and the return. I will review Sean's story in terms of the different parts of the myth.

THE WOUNDING

Chiron was wounded twice. His first wounding came very early in his life when he was abandoned and rejected by his parents. His second wounding, his mortal wounding, came with Hercules' arrow.

The first wounding represents the hurts and scars we all carry by virtue of being human and alive. For Sean these hurts were particularly centered on the loss of his father in his teens. His mortal wounding came with his terminal cancer. His uncontrollable physical pain was a symptom of the latter, unhealable wound, while being also an expression of those earlier, unresolved hurts, now reawakened.

THE STRUGGLE

While to a mortal the poisoned arrow would have been fatal, Chiron was a demigod, therefore he did not die but was condemned instead to a tortured living death. He withdrew into his cave and into himself, and his only journeys out into the world were in an increasingly desperate search to find a cure for his suffering.

The middle part of Sean's story can be seen in this light. Chiron's struggle and its modern medical equivalent, the medical model, are apparent in the attempts made to cure both the cancer and the pain. While initially the positive effects of the cooperation between Sean and the medical team were apparent, in the later stages they became less so. Even though the focus of the struggle was changing from the cancer to the pain, there were still increasingly desperate efforts to "make it all better" and a feeling that those involved were somehow missing the point. Although the causes of Sean's physical problems were accurately diagnosed, the diagnosis was incomplete because it was made from within the limited perspective of the medical model. It is hardly surprising, therefore, that the various treatments given to Sean proved ineffective. Sean was asking for more than he was being offered. His pain had deep psychological and existential roots, but for a considerable time these were not recognized.

THE CHOICE

One day Hercules returned to Chiron and presented him with a possible way out of his suffering. Zeus had decreed that Prometheus, whom he had imprisoned for tricking and insulting him, could be released only if an immortal agreed voluntarily to surrender his immortality and offer himself in place of Prometheus. Chiron chose this path.

While the medical model works for certain individuals even in extreme circumstances where a positive attitude can make all the difference, for others, as for Sean, a time comes when this approach is no longer helpful. A different viewpoint is needed, which involves moving beyond the heroic stance, but for a variety of reasons this is not easily achieved. How can one stop struggling for a cure when, from a medical point of view, it may be difficult to say with certainty that the illness is indeed "terminal" and particularly when the patient is, like Sean, young and desperate to live? Furthermore, how can doctor and patient let go of the struggle if they both believe that this is the only hope, if they do not think there is anything to let go *to,* and if the utter defeat of death appears the only alternative? In my experience as a doctor it is very difficult to discuss this radical change in viewpoint in a positive way with a patient from within the medical model, where such a proposal can look like a suggestion to "throw in the towel." The way I talked to Sean about the potential value of imagework was an attempt to do just this. By describing this approach as a "technique" to help his pain I was using the familiar language of the medical model to gain his cooperation.

The difficulties of such a task can also be seen in mythological terms. What is at stake here is nothing less than Chiron's choosing to surrender his immortality and to step into the unknown. For the patient and caregiver "letting go of immortality" and "stepping into the unknown" must be seen metaphorically rather than literally. "Letting go of immortality" means that both caregiver and patient must choose to let go of the illusion of omnipotence: that they can "fix" the mortal wound, that death is a problem to be solved if we only keep on struggling against it. "Stepping into the unknown" means turning to face what we have been struggling against, the suffering that is our experience of mortal woundedness, and allowing ourselves to descend into the core of such experience.

The implication is not that the struggle generated by the medical model is simply an impediment to be overcome on the path to inner healing. Such a view would be both naive and inaccurate. On the contrary—and this was true for Sean—the struggle is frequently an essential part of the early stages of this process. Sean could not have come to the point of choosing to go with his imagination and cooperate with the way of descent had he not initially fought against it. One could say that it was his courageous struggle which brought him to the edge of his strength, to the edge of all possibilities, and to the edge of his mortal wound, and that this was the place where the choice presented itself. Furthermore, it was in the midst of Sean's struggle, as individual members of the caring team stayed close to him despite the many difficulties and repeated failures, that trust began to develop. This trust, like a small boat on a turbulent sea, created the relatively contained and secure space where choice became a possibility.

The choice that confronted Sean was not, therefore, whether or not to "throw in the towel," but whether or not to listen to his deep inner experience. He decided on the latter by trusting the images which arose from the depths of that experience. The imagework helped to change the focus of his attention and to launch him into depth. By bringing him beneath his denial, it led him beyond his struggle to the very heart of his experience while allowing the protective aspect of the denial to remain intact. It soon became clear that his pain was (onionlike) many-layered. Deeper than his physical pain was his grief for his father and, deeper still, his fear of death.

Sean's story, and others told later in the book, need to be seen in context. In working with those close to death, I have observed that most individuals make the transition from what we have called the heroic stance to the way of descent when they are ready, spontaneously and in their own way, and that they do not need any special psychological intervention to enable them to do so. For them "the choice" is usually unspoken and unseen. The simple and effective care of those around them and, even more important, the silent promptings of their own frail and bone-weary bodies, ease them, as tenderly and naturally as a mother laying down her child, from struggle to descent. Where imagework, or some such depth skill, is of particular value is in creating the circumstances whereby individuals like Sean, who are ripe to make this transition but have become stuck in the process, may be enabled to make the choice which allows this to occur.

Victor Frankl, psychotherapist and survivor of Auschwitz, writes that "everything can be taken from a man but one thing; the last of human freedoms—to choose one's attitude in any given set of circumstances, to choose one's own way." This remark underlines the enormous significance of the moment of choice, the pivotal event in the process of deep inner healing. It marks the paradigm shift whereby the dying individual moves beyond the struggle of the heroic stance into new and uncharted territories through the way of descent.

The Descent

And so Chiron died and descended into the underworld of Tartarus.

In Sean's story this refers not to his literal death but to the metaphorical death which occurred as he moved beyond his struggle and descended into the depths of his experience. His "descent into Tartarus" was his stepping beyond what was known, familiar, and concrete to the underworld of his imagination, a world that was utterly unknown and inhabited by shade-like images. He had descended into dreamtime, but just as in dreams we cannot control what will happen next, this does not mean that we are completely powerless. We are still free to choose the attitude we will adopt to the underworld of our experience. Either we can approach it with the now redundant attitude of the heroic stance, which would plunder, destroy, or simply disregard this deep world of images, or we can adopt a new attitude for this new situation. This is what Sean did.

Sean was utterly present to what he encountered in the depths of his imagination. He noticed, interacted with, and allowed himself to be surprised and educated by its images. In this he was trusting depth, and this in turn enabled the autonomous, healing aspects of depth to begin working on him.

THE RETURN

After nine days in Tartarus, Zeus set Chiron's image among the stars as the constellation Centaurus.

Sean's "return" refers to the subtle change that occurred in him following his descent into the underworld of his imagination. Those close to him in his final weeks felt that he was somehow both profoundly "different" and yet more "himself" than he had ever been. It is this enigmatic sense of transformation, so characteristic of the return, that poet Juan Ramon Jimenez describes with such accuracy in his poem "Oceans" (translated by Robert Bly):

I have a feeling that my boat
has struck, down there in the depths,
against a great thing.
        And nothing
happens! Nothing . . . Silence . . . Waves
—Nothing happens? Or has everything happened,
and are we standing now, quietly, in the new life?

While Sean was not cured in a literal sense by this process, it had led to both quantitative and qualitative changes in his life. The quantitative change meant that he now had less physical pain and became sedated by medications which he had previously easily tolerated. The qualitative change was evident in a new attitude toward his illness and his pain. As his body weakened daily, those close to him noted that he was no longer struggling in anguish and that he had become more peaceful. He no longer spoke of "getting better" and said that while his pain was still there it was "not the same problem it had been." While these changes might be attributed partly to the emotional catharsis and articulation of profound need that occurred when he experienced and expressed his grief for his father, they were also due to his experiencing the healing power of the imagination.

For me, personally, Sean's "return" was particularly evident in the different nature of the contacts I had with him in those final weeks. Whereas previously I had come away from Sean and his overwhelming pain feeling impotent, a failure, guilty, panicky, and drained, I now felt enriched and as though I was learning something very important from him. Whereas before it had most definitely been hero (albeit an unsuccessful one) with victim (albeit a disappointed one), it now felt more like human, who happened to be the doctor, with human, who happened to be the patient. Sean had become a wounded healer, another sure mark of the return.

The Surface and the Deep:
A Psychological Model

Chiron's ultimate healing came with his choice to let go of his immortality. His mortal wound became the gateway to the underworld of Hades through which he chose to descend, aware that the pain had now gone, yet not knowing what would happen next. While the heroic stance prepared for the choice, it was through his cooperation with the way of descent that the healing came.

The above paragraph describes in mythological terms a central dynamic in the dying process, but its potential value and relevance to dying individuals and their caregivers may remain unclear unless these concepts are expressed in a simpler and more accessible way. To this end, a psychological model is necessary to link this ancient knowledge to everyday experience. The challenge is to find a terminology which, while being accurate, will also be acceptable to as wide a group of people as possible. The real test of such a model will be whether or not it makes sense to those caring for people close to death and, even more important, to dying individuals themselves at a time when they may be weak, tired, and frightened. The *surface/deep model* that follows, which is based on descriptions of the human psyche by pioneering depth psychologist Carl Jung, is an attempt to meet this challenge.

The term "surface mind" describes the rational and literal aspects of the mind. This is the dimension of mind from which people typically operate in the normal waking state, as they go about their daily activities and relate to others and their environment. Communication from this dimension of mind is through words which express logical concepts. The strengths of the surface mind are in its ability to analyze and understand.

The "ego" or the "I" is the aware and organizing part of our mind. In terms of the Chiron myth, the ego and Chiron may be seen as one and the same. The ego is at home in the surface mind where it feels safe, as this is familiar territory and things usually work here in predictable and orderly ways. Furthermore, in the surface mind, the ego experiences itself as being in control, and it enjoys this feeling of power. The ego in the surface mind, like Chiron at the peak of the successful first half of his life, operates from the heroic paradigm.

From within the surface mind, the ego views the deep mind with dislike, mistrust, and fear, seeing it as a bottomless pit containing all manner of psychic waste and untamed instincts. This attitude is reminiscent of how Chiron regarded his mortal, animal lower half. In the opinion of the ego, we would be better off without the deep mind, but seeing as we are saddled with it, so to speak, the best we can do is to keep it firmly under lock and key and carry on as if it did not exist. The ego resists entering this unknown terrain as desperately as Chiron struggled against his mortal wound.

The deep mind describes the normally unconscious and intu-

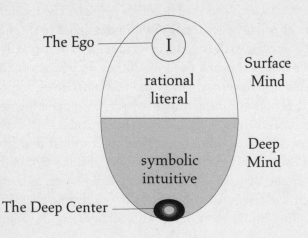

itive aspects of the mind. It is intimately connected to the emotions and the physical body. Its vocabulary is image, symbol, and myth. This is the dimension of mind that is operative in our dreams at night. It may also come to the fore at certain times in the waking state—for example while "daydreaming," while involved in creative activities that engage the imagination, and in certain states of meditation.

The "deep mind" might be seen as a once known but long forgotten ancient place where a different sense of time and causality applies. When the ego enters the deep mind, it has a sense of remembering and of dreaming, and yet, to paraphrase James Hillman, it is unclear if it is the "I" who is remembering or the one who is being remembered, if it is the "I" who is doing the dreaming or the one who is being dreamed. The ego in the deep mind is like Chiron in Tartarus.

While this underworld of consciousness is the "basement" area where old hurts, hates, painful memories, and fears are locked away, there is more to it than that. The deep mind is also the location of great inner resources and childlike spontaneity. Like some enormous subterranean cavern, it contains, often in the most unlikely and darkest corners and in the most unexpected of disguises, exactly what is needed to deal with the particular question, challenge, or life crisis that confronts us. Like an aboriginal dreamland, it is a place of paradox whose riches are accessible only to those who are actually prepared to go there.

The "deep center" is how anthropologist Peter Martin describes what at the core of our being is ultimately unnameable, that which is deepest in us, the essence of who we are. It corresponds to what Jung calls the Self, and is closely linked with what is universally known as spirit. It is the royal ruler in the depths of the human psyche, the alchemist who, working in the very heart of darkness, can transform the most ordinary and painful human experiences into gold. This is Zeus's thunderbolt which pierced the darkness of Hades and initiated Chiron's return.

Soul

Throughout this book, I use the term "soul pain" to describe a particular type of suffering which may be experienced by those close to death. Before considering in more detail the nature and origins of soul pain and beginning to explore possible ways of responding to the challenge it presents, I want to pause to consider what is meant by "soul."

For many, the word "soul" may have religious connotations and be understood as some vague and ethereal phantasm that is somehow in opposition to the physical and earthy part of ourselves and more likely to be at home in the "next world" than in this. I am using "soul" in its more classical sense as referring to "psyche." In contrast to the religious polarization of soul from body, soul as psyche is at the very heart of, and at one with, human experience. To describe a person as "soulful," therefore, is not to describe someone who has transcended their humanity but one who is filled with the flesh and feeling of the world.

My mentor in the ways of soul has been the archetypal psychologist James Hillman. In his writings Hillman frequently comments that soul as psyche is that in us which experiences and is experienced imaginatively, emotionally, and physically rather than rationally grasped or understood. "Soul," he elaborates, "sticks to the realm of experience and to reflections within experience. It moves indirectly in circular reasonings, where retreats are as important as advances, preferring labyrinths and corners, giving a metaphorical sense to life through such words as *close, near, slow,* and *deep.* Soul involves us in the pack and welter of phenomena and the flow of impressions. It is the "patient" part of us. Soul is vulnerable and suffers; it is passive and remembers. It is water to the spirit's fire, like a mermaid who beckons the heroic spirit into the depths of passions to extinguish its certainty." While emphasizing that soul defies definition, Hillman states that there are, nonetheless, certain things that can be said about it.

First, to speak of soul is to speak of depth, for soul refers to "the *deepening* of events into experience." Hillman quotes a fragment from the ancient Greek philosopher Heraclitus, that "you could not discover the limits of soul (psyche), even if you travelled every road to do so; such is the depth (bathun) of its meaning" and writes that "the dimension of soul is depth (not breadth or height) and the dimension of soul travel is downward." This quotation from Heraclitus also connects soul and depth with meaning, for soul brings with it a sense of significance, that is, *a subjective experience of meaning,* which is an altogether different thing from the rational mind's preoccupation with extracting meaning from experience.

Second, Hillman says, "the significance soul makes possible . . . derives from its *special relation with death.*" In his book *The Dream and the Underworld* he explores in detail the relationship between soul as depth and the underworld of mind, and the ancient Greek idea of the underworld of Hades, the realm of death. He quotes Jung as saying that "the dread and resistance which every natural human being experiences when it comes to delving too deeply into himself is, at bottom, the fear of the journey to Hades." That is, our instinctive fear and resistance to the dark and unknown depths of psyche is one and the same as our fear of death. Third, Hillman says, "*soul is imagination,*" that is, soul is "the imaginative possibility in our natures, the experiencing through reflective speculation, dream, image and *fantasy*—that mode which recognises all realities as primarily symbolic and metaphorical."

My own personal and work experience has repeatedly endorsed these observations of Hillman's, that soul is indeed connected to depth, to death, to the imagination, and that it brings with it a sense of meaning. These characteristics of soul were beautifully expressed to me some years ago by the relative of a man who had died in the hospice. This man, whose name was Eamonn, was someone who had come very slowly and painfully to a place of inner peace and wholeness during his final weeks. I believe that his sister's attempt to describe the subtle yet definite change she experienced in Eamonn, written in a letter which I received after his death, is also a graphic portrait of soul: "As I remember how he was shortly before his death, I can't help thinking of Rembrandt's paintings, where the light is so glorious that it makes even the darkness look beautiful. I can't put it any better than that, except perhaps one could say that the light only looked so glorious *because* of the darkness around it. The darkness was the cause of the beauty, not so much the light."

In terms of the surface deep model, what we can say of soul, therefore, is similar to much we have already said of the deep mind but with one important exception. Soul is not some inanimate thing nor yet some region in the topography of the mind. Soul is a dynamic entity, often personified in feminine form, which, while being at home in the deep mind, is constantly moving back and forth between the surface and the deep, weaving a web of images in a restless longing to bring depth to all that is superficial and to bring what is superficial into depth. Soul is the living connection between the surface and the unfathomable and meaning-rich depths of who we are.

Soul Pain

A move from the surface to the deep mind is a psychological way of describing the radical paradigm shift involved in Chiron's changing from the heroic stance to the way of descent. This shift is pivotal in the dying process, and a lot depends on whether it occurs and how and when it does so. If this downward movement does occur—and this happens for the majority of individuals naturally, quietly, invisibly, and in its own time and way—such individuals experience a new peace, a richness, and a depth in their living and their dying. They have come into the meaning of soul.

For others, however, this spontaneous descent does not happen, and these individuals remain trapped at the surface level of their mind, cut off from the healing power of their own inner depths. While in mythological terms this corresponds to Chiron's struggling to escape from the agony of his mortal wound, in psychological terms it is a symptom of the ego's total identification with the surface mind and its resistance to a descent into depth. This results in *soul pain*, which is *the experience of an individual who has become disconnected and alienated from the deepest and most fundamental aspects of himself or herself.*

There is a variety of reasons why this move from the surface to the deep mind is resisted, hampered, or blocked. One of these is that the ego is proud and has a deluded sense of its own omnipotence. Such a move appears to the ego as a disaster, a defeat, the worst possible scenario, the end, and is, therefore, utterly unacceptable. Another is that the ego is terrified of death. The ego sees and believes in what is literal, familiar, and tangible and it likes above all else to be in control. Death, therefore, the utterly unfamiliar and uncontrollable unknown, poses the ultimate threat to the ego. The ego has a finely tuned nose for death and can smell its approach when it is still many miles away. This triggers one or both basic ego survival reactions of "fight" and "flight."

While the fight and flight reactions are most apparent at a surface level in all the individual does to "beat" and "cope with" the illness, there is also an inner and deeper dimension to these survival reactions that is relevant here. To the ego, the unknowable depths of soul are seen as a microcosm of death. And so, as death approaches, the frantic ego will sometimes project its fear of literal death onto metaphorical death—that is, the inner underworld, the enemy within, depth itself. The "fight" then becomes a devaluing of all that is soul—"Forget that dream rubbish, cure is the only reality that matters now!" screams the ego—while the "flight" is seen in an ever upward retreat to the reassuring safety of rationality. The writer and artist D. H. Lawrence describes this graphically in the following lines, in which he refers to the ego as the "timid soul":

Piecemeal the body dies, and the timid soul
has her footing washed away, as the dark flood rises.

We are dying, we are dying, we are all of us dying
and nothing will stay the death-flood rising within us
and soon it will rise on the world, on the outside world.

We are dying, we are dying, piecemeal our bodies are dying
and our strength leaves us,
and our soul cowers naked in the dark rain over the flood,
cowering in the last branches of the tree of our life.

While it is understandable that the ego might fear and resist a move from the daylight of the surface to the dark depths of soul, in a certain sense there is no choice. Like it or not, as Lawrence says, "we are all of us dying and nothing will stay the death-flood rising within us." One day death will bring each of us into depth. The choice is not whether or not we go, but how we go. If we resist this descent, the dying process may become a time of escalating fear and suffering, as for someone in a trapped place whose supply of oxygen is dwindling. If, when the moment is ripe, we choose to go willingly with this inner gravity, a new way may surprisingly open up to us.

Soul pain in another can be recognized in a number of ways. First, we tend to use a characteristic vocabulary in our attempts to describe such an individual's distress. We may find ourselves using words like "suffering," "anguished," or "tortured," as we frequently did in speaking of Jackie or Sean. Second, because the physical body is intimately connected with the psyche, soul pain will often manifest physically as symptoms that do not respond to usually successful forms of treatment, as was again the case with Jackie's and Sean's physical pain. Third, as these individuals' stories also illustrate, soul pain can find expression emotionally as fear and behaviorally as the "fight" of an agitated struggle to find a way out of the awful situation, in impossible demands of the caregivers to "*do* something, anything—can't you see I'm in agony," or as the "flight" of psychological denial. Finally, because soul pain results from an alienation from the deepest aspects of ourselves, there may be an all-pervading sense of emptiness, hopelessness, and meaninglessness.

Soul pain can also be recognized by the feelings and behavior patterns it awakens or "constellates" in us as caregivers. In the presence of soul pain, we too are confronted by an insoluble problem. This pain which we cannot control triggers our own ego survival reactions. At a surface level, we too "fight," that is, we never give up: we continue to try new treatments or administer bigger and bigger doses of painkillers and tranquilizers. In other words, we *do*, we *do*, and even when we do not succeed, we *go on doing*. Alternatively, or simultaneously, our attempts at "flight" may become apparent in our attempts to get out of this painful situation as quickly as possible. This usually takes the form of an urgent referral to the social worker, counselor, or chaplain who are, we claim, "better suited than we are to deal with this type of problem." Simultaneously, in our inner world, we can also become disconnected from depth and experience soul pain. As we go numb from the neck down, our mind knows with absolute clarity that we do not have the answer for this person's pain, but at that moment we feel nothing. It is later on that we experience feelings, and in particular a sense of guilt and shame. We know that we have failed to give that person what they really needed from us. In some way we know that in allowing ourselves to be dominated by these survival reactions, we have colluded in denial with the person in pain, and our sense of failure is compounded by our knowing, instinctively, that an act of double betrayal has taken place.

In considering how we might respond to someone in soul pain, the term itself offers us an important clue. Soul points us inward and downward to the roots of our humanity and suggests that reconnection with depth is the central issue.

We must start with the symptoms—physical, emotional, and social—which are troubling the dying individual and do all we can to ease them. That is, we must begin with good palliative care and use this expertise to achieve physical comfort, to open up blocked channels of communication, and to provide emotional and social support.

In terms of the model I have just developed, this work might be called *surface work*. "Surface," used in this way, does not mean "superficial," nor intend a value judgment. On the contrary, the surface is the way to the deep, and surface work is the necessary first step in that direction. For many, this will be enough to create the containment they needed to silently commit themselves to their inner descent; for others, it will only be the beginning. *Depth work*, on the other hand, might be described as any approach or intervention that brings an individual into an experience of soul.

It is somewhat artificial to talk of surface and depth work in this way, as if they were two completely distinct and separate entities, because, much of the time, caring, effective surface work is itself midwife to depth. As Saunders says, "The way care is given can reach the most hidden places," reminding us that what we do at a surface level can make all the difference. Our own relationship to depth, as caregivers, also matters hugely. The individual in soul pain knows intuitively if the person beside them is someone familiar with depth and beloved of soul. Such a caregiver can bring reassurance to that person and encourage their own letting go to soul. Depth work is also about reconnecting with those very simple and very ordinary aspects of life that have, in the past, brought us a sense of depth or significance; what Kreinheder calls "meaningful things done meaningfully." This might involve the sharing of old memories, spending time with people we love, visiting a place of special importance, returning home from the hospital or, if this is not possible, bringing something we value—a photograph, a particular object, our dog!—into the hospital.

For some, however, the surface and depth work that is good palliative care is not enough. Sean's story and those that follow tell of individuals who, despite such care, remained in soul pain. Here something more was needed, some type of specific intervention which could induce them into the deeper levels of their experience. Imagework is just one example of such a *depth skill*. Others include dream work, art therapy, music therapy, reminiscence and biography therapy, bodywork (including massage), and certain forms of meditation. What all these approaches have in common is that they enable the individual to move, temporarily, into depth.

Two important assumptions underlie these interventions. The first is that the dynamic core of the suffering that is soul pain lies in the terrified ego's resistance to depth. Therefore, if our intervention allows that person to make the descent into depth, as microcosm of death, in a way that feels safe and contained, it may lead to that individual's emerging from the experience less frightened of depth and with less terror of death. Second, if, through these approaches, we can enable that individual to move toward depth, soul itself will act, for there is in depth an autonomy that desires our deepest healing, if only we can allow it to happen.

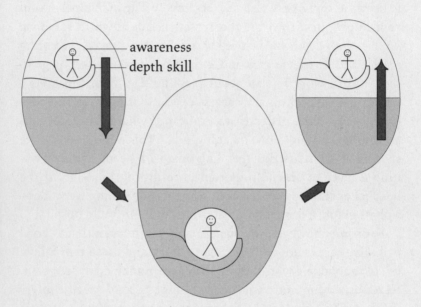

Finally, a word of warning, for there is also danger here. Unless we respect soul as unfathomable and see these approaches simply as a means to create the conditions where soul may do her work, the heroic ego can all too easily take over and, hijacking these techniques, use them to colonize depth and feed the illusion of its own omnipotence. While such tactics may bring temporary success, they will ultimately not help the person in soul pain. On the contrary, they will compound rather than allay that person's fear and store up trouble for the future.

PART 3

MODERN MYTHS

The deep parts of my life pour onward,
as if the river shores were opening out.
It seems that things are more like me now,
that I can see farther into paintings.
I feel closer to what language can't reach.
With my senses, as with birds, I climb
into the windy heaven, out of the oak,
and in the ponds broken off from the sky
my feeling sinks, as if standing on fishes.

RAINER MARIA RILKE, "Moving Forward"
(translated by Robert Bly)

The stories that follow are modern myths. Each has been chosen to illustrate certain aspects of soul pain, although they are by no means an attempt to be exhaustive in this regard. In each instance I initially narrate events as they unfolded, from my perspective as a doctor involved in that person's care, and subsequently reflect on these events in the light of the mythological and psychological models I discussed in Part 2.

In these stories there are descriptions of a number of different imagework exercises which I have developed specifically for individuals close to death. These are recorded in some detail to give the reader further insight into this particular way of working and as a means of providing an insight into what may occur deep in a person's psyche at this critical time. It is not intended that readers should experiment with these exercises on the basis of what they read here. The apparent simplicity of this technique could be deceptive and does not mean that it is harmless. While it is a simple psychotherapeutic tool, it can be extremely powerful and, in my experience, especially so when death is imminent. I would strongly recommend that anyone wishing to use imagework as a depth skill should first undergo the necessary training and arrange supervision with a psychotherapist familiar with this approach.

From Fear to Sadness:
Dara's Story

When I think of Dara, I feel sad and guilty, for here is a story without a happy ending. I tell it because Dara said I could do so, and because it brings some insight into the nature of extreme fear in the face of death.

I remember sitting on the edge of Dara's bed and wondering what I could possibly do next. It was early December and at this stage Dara had already been in the hospice for almost two weeks. He was forty years old, and although he was a physical wreck, there was something youthful in his eyes. The cancer in the lymph nodes at the side of his neck had caused swelling and twisting of his mouth, distorting his face. His long hair showed a bohemian streak but looked bedraggled alongside his gaunt and frightened face. Because he had had major surgery to remove the primary cancer in his larynx, he could no longer speak. He tried to communicate by using a special microphone which he held to the underside of his chin, where it picked up the vibrations when he spoke and amplified them as a coarse whisper. Unfortunately, this never seemed to work as it should for Dara, but he was not willing to accept this and pressed on regardless, while frustration built up on all sides.

Dara was an artist and a skilled jazz musician. He lived in the basement of a house belonging to a female friend, Crostella, where the home care team from the hospice had visited him for some weeks. They had been asked in by his family doctor, who was having difficulty in controlling his pain. Despite using very large doses of morphine and other, usually reliable, medications, they too found it hard to control his pain. All those involved, including Dara and Crostella, agreed that fear was a major component in his problems, and his admission to the hospice was arranged to optimize physical treatments for pain while using other approaches to try to lessen the fear.

Shortly after Dara's arrival in the hospice, the admitting doctor asked him what he felt his major concerns were. Dara, who was fully aware of the nature and extent of his illness at this stage, did not indicate his pain, or his increasing difficulty in swallowing, but put the special microphone under his chin and, in a voice that was barely comprehensible, croaked that he was "terrified to death."

Dara's first two weeks in the hospice did not go well. Within his first forty-eight hours in the ward, the two men who had been sharing the four-bedded ward with him died. For many, witnessing death in this way, particularly a death that is peaceful and obviously free of pain, can be a reassurance and a comfort, but for Dara it seemed to have the opposite effect. He became agitated and unsettled, and his nights were particularly disturbed. By day he was drowsy because of an accumulation of night sedation, but he still managed to tell us that despite the changes we had made in his treatment, the pain was no better and his swallowing was definitely worse.

Toward the end of Dara's first week in the hospice we offered him a single room, as we felt that this might suit him better. He readily accepted this. His fear had by then become more apparent, and it was evident that any possible reassurance that might have come from the company of the open ward was being negated by his being in contact with others iller than he was. In addition, we felt that the worsening problem of communication would be easier to deal with in the privacy of a quieter space.

By the end of the second week we, as a ward team, had to accept that things had not improved for Dara. His nights were still very unsettled despite strong night sedation and the presence of a nurse to sit with him. By day, it was apparent that his physical condition was worsening. He was weak and drowsy, and his swallowing was intermittently obstructed. As speech had by now become impossible for him, Dara communicated by writing notes. When I asked him if he could name any particular fears, he immediately wrote that he was particularly terrified of the possibility of choking. I told him that whatever developed, we would never allow this to happen. Although in the immediate aftermath of this exchange he seemed a little calmer, his agitation that night, which continued unabated into the following day, made it clear that I had not succeeded in reassuring him. We decided then that it might help to work more at a nonverbal level and offered Dara aromatherapy massage. However, while it was obvious that he relaxed during the sessions and enjoyed them, these were brief respites, and within hours he was again anxious, restless, and afraid.

We then convened a case conference to discuss Dara's situation. As a team we shared the view that we had failed to help him. During those first few difficult weeks that Dara spent in the hospice, some of the nurses had become particularly close to him, and were pained and angry at our impotence to allay his fear and truly comfort him. What were we to do? We saw few options. One was to treat his overwhelming emotional distress as though it were a physical pain, by numbing it with increasing doses of tranquilizing medication. We decided against this because any further increase in his medication would probably lead to complete sedation. While this might have eased our distress, it was evident from his frequent complaints about his current levels of drowsiness that it was not what Dara himself wanted. We opted instead to continue in the same manner for the immediate future, accepting that we might never "win" in this situation. This meant that we had to accept that Dara's fear was probably more than we with our collective skills and goodwill could deal with. We, nonetheless, continued to hope that time, more realistic expectations of ourselves, and a continued growth in the trust that was developing between Dara and certain members of the team would make a difference. Meanwhile, we agreed to meet Dara's sister, Aifric, and Crostella to brief them and hear their views. I was also to meet Dara to see if he might be interested and willing to do some imagework.

As I entered his room, greeted him, and sat on the edge of his bed, I noticed that he was drowsy and yet he could not lie still. He sat forward, reached for something on his bedside locker, lay back, turned to face me, and then turned the other way. And so it continued. When I asked him how he was feeling, he mumbled an answer I could not understand and then scribbled a note that I found illegible. "Dara," I said, "there is something I want to put to you." This caught his attention, and for the first time he rested back on his pillows and closed his eyes. I told him that I would like him to do a type of visualization exercise and that I hoped this would make him feel less anxious and more relaxed. I explained what it would entail and emphasized that he was free to open his eyes and end the exercise at any time he wished. He opened his eyes at this point and indicated, by nodding his head, that he was willing to go ahead.

I had decided to do some guided imagery with Dara, along similar lines to what I had done with Sean. Whereas normally I would build a number of pauses into an exercise such as this to check how the person was getting on and to hear what images were coming up for them, because of the communication difficulties here, I decided in this instance to run the visualization straight through from beginning to end and take time to discuss it together afterward.

By the end of the introductory part of the exercise, Dara already looked more relaxed. I asked him to imagine himself standing on a sandy beach by a lakeside. It was a sunny day with a blue sky, and the lake water was calm. There was no one else around, but when he looked down along the beach he saw a little wooden rowboat at the water's edge, its oars resting in the oarlocks. I suggested that he could borrow the boat if he wished. As he pushed the boat out into the lake, he fitted the oars in place and began to row. All he was aware of was the noise of the lake water as the oars dipped in and out. Soon he was far out, the beach behind him now a thin golden band. He was hot from the sun and the rowing, and I suggested that he might like to let himself over the side and into the cool water of the lake, but I emphasized that this was a choice for himself. If he did so, I asked him to notice how he felt and anything particular that happened. After a pause of a minute or so, I asked him, if he had got into the water, to get back into the boat and then to continue rowing toward a beach which was not far off, on the far side of the lake. As he looked over his shoulder to see if he was heading in the right direction, he noticed that there was a person on the beach who seemed to be waiting for him. He knew that this person was someone wise and loving who had come here today because he or she cared deeply about him and wanted to help him in any way possible. As he came nearer to the beach he could make out the features of this person, perhaps someone familiar to him or perhaps a stranger. In any case, he knew that this person wished him well and that when he got ashore he could voice his deepest feelings to this person and ask for any help he needed. At this point Dara opened his eyes and looked at me. I asked him if he would like to stop there to discuss what had come up for him, and he nodded.

Handing Dara his writing pad, I asked him to describe what had happened as he did the exercise. He began to draw a little sailboat in a vast expanse of sea. In the middle foreground he drew a picture of a man in the water, who was locked in a desperate battle with an enormous sharklike fish. He indicated that the shark had come up from behind him and had taken a chunk out of his right shoulder. He had a pistol on his right hip and a sword in his right hand which he had managed to stick into the

shark. At that he paused, sat back, and looked at me. I asked him to describe his feelings during all this. "Fear . . . terror . . . panic," he wrote. "And the wise and loving person on the shore, did you get a sense of such a person and who that might be?" I asked. Returning to his picture he began to draw this person in the near foreground, standing on the beach. It was a woman who was facing out toward the water, and she had both hands raised above her head, as if waving to get his attention. When he had finished drawing her, he wrote CRO . . . CRO on her back, indicating that this was his friend, Crostella. "And did you get a sense of what it was you needed and wanted to ask from this person?" I asked. He gestured a hug by wrapping his arms around himself, and he then began to cry.

Immediately after this session there was a noticeable change in Dara, and this lasted through the following five days. The feelings of tension and panic in his room were replaced by a sense of profound sadness. He wanted both Aifric and Crostella to be with him all the time, and when they were there he was soft and affectionate and tearful with them and wanted to be held and comforted. As the fear was no longer apparent, we were able to dramatically reduce his medications. He became more alert, and communication was easier.

Unfortunately, the situation changed over the following weekend. Dara's fear returned with a new ferocity and was now accompanied by paranoia. He believed that we in the hospice were trying to kill him and demanded that we allow him to return home. He said this to his family and friends, but they replied that even though they would like that too, they simply could not give him the level of care he now needed. While we fully supported them in this decision, they spoke of feeling guilty that they were failing Dara when he most needed them.

Reluctantly, following a lengthy discussion with his family, we decided that we once again needed to increase Dara's sedation. He slept well that night and was still very drowsy when I went in to see him the following morning. I asked him how he was. He reached for his writing pad and drew what looked a bit like a sinking boat. He then became agitated and scribbled that I was trying to kill him, that he did not want me to visit him from then on and would like the other doctor on our team to take over his care. Over the next twenty-four hours he became progressively more distressed and restless, and we felt we had no option but to further increase his sedation. Within hours of this Dara settled into a calm sleep. Overnight, however, his chest became congested, his condition weakened, and he died early the following morning.

What is it in me that does not find it easy to remember, let alone tell, this sad story? I believe it is my wounded heroic pride, that in me in which Dara placed so much trust in his final weeks and days, the hero who failed in his task to "make it all better."

There are obviously a lot of similarities between Dara's and Sean's stories. Here were two young men who did not want to die, who fought desperately against death and who experienced great soul pain, as well as other kinds of suffering, in the process. In both situations the soul pain initially manifested itself as physical symptoms, the deeper source of their distress becoming evident only over time as normally successful treatments failed to make an impact and additional characteristic features of soul pain began to appear. In Sean's case, because of his emotional denial, the soul pain remained to some extent somaticized, that is, expressed as physical symptoms, until the very end. By contrast, in Dara's case, in the absence of denial, the soul pain stepped nakedly out from behind the mask of his physical symptoms, declaring itself as undiluted terror.

Another feature common to Dara's and Sean's stories is the response their distress elicited in me and other members of the caring team. We have already discussed how the guiding paradigm of the medical profession is the heroic medical model, the motto of which might read, "We shall (always) overcome. Just give us time and your complete and unquestioning trust." It is not surprising, therefore, that this should remain the basis of the unspoken contract at the heart of all medical care, even at the very end of life. This is not said by way of apology, as we have already seen some of the potential benefits of the heroic approach even in the presence of death, but to identify the heroic stance as the dominant paradigm of those early days as we struggled to help Dara.

Just as analgesic medication was helpful in treating Sean's physical pain, so too there was, I believe, a place for using tranquilizing or sedative medication in our attempts to ease Dara's emotional pain. By lessening the intensity of an individual's distress, such medication can help to create a more secure environment, enabling that individual to come out of isolation into relationship with others and with the deeper levels of his or her own experience. Pharmacological treatment of emotional distress, therefore, should be seen as a symptomatic and containing measure and just one step in an ongoing process, rather than as an end in itself. We must, however, be cautious here. In using tranquilizing medication, the caregivers may also be motivated by the desire to ease the pain of their own bruised heroic ego, now facing defeat. This can all too easily lead to an excessive use of these drugs, resulting in oversedated and uncomplaining patients. While this type of intervention is justified as being necessary for the patient's well-being, which it may or may not be in any particular instance, such an approach is open to abuse if the caregivers fail to recognize and accept that such treatment is also palliating their own distress.

Dara was terrified of death. As an artist and "sensitive soul" he may not only have been more in touch with his own personal feeling world than most individuals, but may have been picking up the feelings of those around him, and possibly even some of the collective feelings toward death that are present at a cultural level. Certainly there was a sense among Dara's caregivers that his fear was *enormous,* as well as being palpable and contagious, and undoubtedly this fired our efforts to search for a solution on his behalf. It seems just as likely that the contagion was working both ways and that Dara was simultaneously picking up the feelings of frustration and panic of those who surrounded him at that time.

My offering to do imagework with Dara was a further heroic gesture, in that my intention was clearly to initiate something that might lessen his distress. However, that depth work is a heroic intervention with a difference is evident in the paradox it presented to Dara. In terms of the Chiron myth, there are parallels here to Hercules' returning to the wounded centaur with the suggestion that he swap places with Prometheus. Rather than saying, "Relax, I will help you to escape from what chases you," I was challenging Dara to "Stop, turn around, face your fear, and begin to walk toward it."

Dara, at this point, was in emotional crisis. These were certainly not the ideal circumstances in which to do depth work, and there were risks involved in proceeding with the imagework at this time. For example, it might have triggered a flooding of consciousness by previously suppressed unconscious emotion, which would have exacerbated his sense of not being in control and made him even more frightened. I chose to go ahead, nonetheless, for two reasons. First, because short of further increasing his sedative medication I and the rest of the team caring for him did not see any other treatment alternatives and, second, because I believed that beneath his emotional turmoil there was another part of him that was not afraid; that somewhere deep inside him was a source of strength and comfort and that this approach offered a real chance for him to access this. An interesting detail is that Dara participated in the imagework session at a time when he was still on strong doses of tranquilizing medication, demonstrating that psychologically active drugs do not necessarily impede the workings of the imagination.

There is something both valiant and accurate in Dara's image of the man locked in mortal combat with the sharklike fish. It is happening near the surface and closely resembles Chiron's heroic struggle against the forces that were trying to pull him into depth. This is a terrifying moment, and literally a struggle to the death. In imagining it in this way, Dara was giving face to his greatest fear. Then came the intervention of helping him to look in another direction, toward the shore where someone who was wise and loving waited for him. There he saw his dear friend Crostella whose presence spoke of that in him which wished him well and was there with him as witness and ally even in this, his loneliest moment. In shifting his attention from the struggle to the shore Dara realized that he was not alone.

The dramatic change in Dara following this session offers an insight into emotional aspects of the struggle and the descent. Fear is the primary emotion of the surface struggle for survival and is often associated with the agitated and restless behavior of one desperate to find an escape. This fear had dominated Dara in the preceding weeks. His choosing to participate in the image-work session brought him to the threshold of a new emotional territory. He crossed this threshold the moment he recognized, beyond his fear, the face of one who cared for him. At that moment, fear loosened its grip and, instead of clutching a sword and holding an attacking shark at bay, his arms could now enfold his own fragile body. Dara had moved from the struggle to the way of descent. The emotions that accompany the descent are the many emotions of grief, primary among which is sadness, and it was this fathomless and inconsolable sadness that filled his room during those days.

Dara's relapse into frightened confusion just before he died is a reminder that despite our best efforts, and perhaps because an individual's soul pain is occasionally more than a purely personal issue, we cannot always achieve what we would like for that person. It also shows the limited potential of imagework in extreme situations such as this, where so much is left so late. Finally, Dara's paranoia, his seeing me at that time as someone who was trying to kill him, may have been his ego's literalist misinterpretation of my attempts to help him to move from his surface prison to what I hoped would be the freedom of the underworld of depth.

The Pain of No Meaning:
Frank's Story

Frank was a seventy-year-old man who was admitted to the hospice because his family, friends, and professional caregivers had been unable to ease his great emotional distress. Just over a year previously he had had major surgery to remove a cancerous growth from his right lung. In recent weeks he had begun to lose weight, despite eating well, and had been having drenching night-sweats. Because of a new pain in his ribs, his family doctor had recently arranged an X ray of Frank's chest. This revealed that the cancer had recurred in the lymph nodes in the center of his chest and had also spread to a number of ribs.

Despite having had several meetings with his family doctor since then, Frank had never asked for the results of the X ray. This was felt to be a significant change in his behavior, given his previous insistence on knowing every detail of what was going on with his illness and treatment. Instead, Frank began to complain of feeling "awful." Those who listened to him at that time quickly sensed that what he meant by this was something more than the effect of his troublesome physical symptoms. Frank was an intelligent and articulate man, but he still had to struggle to find words for how he was feeling. Eventually, he settled on the words "depressed," "bored," and "hopeless." His family doctor believed these feelings were symptoms of an acute depression brought on by the stress and uncertainty of his situation and prescribed antidepressant medication. However, Frank showed no signs of improvement in the weeks that followed, which is what prompted his caregivers to suggest a respite admission to the hospice.

As I sat with Frank in his room a week or so after his admission, he began to express feelings of disappointment. He had come in with high expectations, having heard such "great things about the hospice." True, we had managed to ease some of his physical symptoms, and in particular his pain and night-sweats had responded to the treatment we had given him, but it was evident that this did not bring much consolation to him. Frank was obviously still overwhelmed by this sense of "awfulness."

"I just feel terrible," he said. "I've never in my life felt like this before. I realize that I've not been well, but this feeling is worse than any physical pain. It just seems like there's no point to my waking up in the morning; no point in going through the motions of another day. I know that you are all trying to help me, and you're all very nice, but it's been no use. Nothing helps. Even when I pause to catch breath, this feeling catches up with me. It's like a voice that mocks me, saying that I may as well just not bother, because nothing matters anymore and nothing anyone does will make the slightest difference. If it goes on like this I would rather be dead. To be honest, doctor, I've even been thinking of doing something to end it all in the last few days. It's that bad. What's stopping me is that I would be worried about the effect this might have on my wife and besides, I am too much of a coward, and that goes for what might be waiting for me on the other side also. I had such high hopes coming in here. Is there nothing else you can do to help me?"

As I listened to this deeply troubled man, I knew that it would be pointless to try, yet again, to find words of comfort or reassurance. These had been offered in abundance by myself and others in the team in recent days but had seemed merely to add salt to his open wound. I decided instead to offer Frank the opportunity of exploring his experience nonverbally, through imagery. I talked to him about imagework, describing it as a technique that might help him feel a little easier in himself. He immediately agreed, and we decided to go ahead with a session later that day.

When I called back to see Frank that afternoon, he was lying on the bed in his single room. Having explained in detail what was involved in the imagework exercise, I emphasized that all the way through the exercise, he could choose whether or not to continue. If he wished, he could open his eyes at any moment and we could talk. Frank seemed happy with this and we agreed to proceed.

Having invited him to close his eyes and having brought him through a relaxation meditation, I asked him if he was aware of that "awful" feeling he had spoken so much of in recent weeks. "Yes," he replied without a moment's hesitation. I asked him to focus his attention on that feeling, to notice where in his body it seemed to be located, its shape, its texture, its tone, and then to give it space, to amplify it in his awareness. I asked him, while staying in touch with this feeling, to allow an image to form in his mind's eye which would show him something he needed to see. At that he began to describe the feeling itself, struggling to find words that might convey its awfulness and to find explanations for what had caused it and what he thought might help.

I decided to try a different approach. Asking Frank to keep his eyes closed, I asked him to picture, in his imagination, a cottage. "Can you see a cottage, Frank?"

"Yes," he replied, "it's got cream walls and a thatched roof and it's in a valley, somewhere in the west of Ireland."

"And what feelings do you experience as you look at this cottage?" I asked.

"Peaceful, calm, dreamlike," he replied.

I asked him to imagine himself standing in the doorway of the cottage, and to look out from there and notice himself standing nearby. "How does Frank appear to you as you look at him in this way?" I asked.

"Weary, gray, lonely," he said.

I invited him once again to locate himself outside the cottage while looking across at it, and suggested to him that in that cottage was someone wise and loving, someone who knew his story, someone who deeply cared about and understood him.

"I know who it is," he interrupted. "It's Joe, an old man from the west of Ireland who used to live near me here in Dublin. He died last year. Joe was someone who said little but who understood." I suggested that Joe then came to the door of the cottage and that Frank could see him standing there. Joe invited him to come in to have a cup of tea and a chat with him by the fire. The choice was his whether or not to accept this invitation. At this, Frank said he wanted to go in.

"As you sit with Joe, you can tell him how you are feeling these times and what it is you need," I said.

"I feel so alone, Joe," Frank said, talking into space, his eyes still closed. "This is all new to me. I need to be understood." Frank then became very still and silent and remained so for several minutes.

Then I asked, "Can you describe what's happening, Frank?"

"Joe is silent," he said. "He listened to me and he put his hand on mine."

After a little while I reached across and put my hand on his and said, "Let this in, Frank, this gesture of solidarity from Joe. Open to how this feels, let it in, Allow it." A few minutes later I asked him to say his good-byes to Joe for now, knowing this place was there for him to visit again if he so wished, and to begin to leave this scene and to come back to the here and now and when he was ready, to open his eyes.

That night Frank appeared to sleep well. When I visited him the following morning I asked him how he was. "I feel a little easier in myself," he replied, "more reconciled." I thought he looked better and noticed that he was no longer as sweaty and pale as he had been.

Frank remained relaxed and comfortable throughout the following days. When I called in to see him toward the end of that week, however, he began to describe a "nightmare" he had had the previous night. "I woke up suddenly. I was in my room here. It was as though I had been asleep for a very long time. Slowly, I realized that I was trapped here, a prisoner. The room was dimly lit by moonlight coming through my window. I began to realize that I was not alone. Over by the corner, where it was particularly dark, there were four people. They were Russians, and they were both alien and somehow intimately familiar to me, as if they were part of me. They were members of some ballet group. It seemed that we were in some way allies and that it was important that their true identity remain unknown. If their identities became known, we would all be sunk." The dream had continued along the same lines and had ended with Frank's feeling that he must get out of bed. When he awoke he was standing beside his bed, looking into the concerned face of the night nurse.

I suggested that it might be valuable for us to take some time to mull over this dream together. Frank agreed, and when he had relaxed on his bed with his eyes closed I asked him to remember the content and the texture of the dream. I asked him what feelings were evoked by his remembering his dream in this way. "Fear and anxiety," he said. I then asked him to reconnect with whatever part of the dream felt most relevant to him. He spoke again of the encounter with the Russian dancers. I encouraged him to reenter that particular sequence as an active participant and to notice what happened. For several minutes he was silent. He then opened his eyes and began to speak of how urgent it was that the Russians' identity remain unknown; "a matter of life and death." He had said to them, "Be careful—don't let them discover who you are or we'll all be trapped." He described their faces as they watched him as being "full of wonder," as though he was simultaneously "a stranger and yet familiar to them." They asked him what would happen if they were discovered. He replied, "I'd be trapped here forever." He said that he had felt absolutely terrified at that moment. They asked him what, above all else, it was that he needed from them. "To be believed," he had answered, to which they had replied, "We believe you, we believe you and we will not forget you." I suggested that he take a minute to stay with these words and whatever feelings they evoked.

Afterward, Frank and I discussed how all this might relate to his current situation. He said that the trapped feeling was very familiar to him from recent weeks and that he sensed the importance of the Russians' identity remaining unknown was related to his own sense of uncertainty about his diagnosis and prognosis. He then surprised me by turning to me and saying, "I feel I might be helped if I knew more clearly what is happening and likely to happen." Then, changing the subject, he began to reflect again on their final words of reassurance. He said, "It was like they were saying they would be with me whatever happens . . . it felt like it was God talking." We ended this meeting by agreeing that I would gather together all the information I could about his illness and come back to him as soon as possible.

When I returned later that day I told him that his cancer had indeed recurred and that his condition was slowly deteriorating. His disappointment was tangible. I added that I too was bitterly disappointed that there was not more I could do for him, but reassured him that he had a place with us as long as he wished, and that I and the rest of the team would continue to do all we could to help him. "Isn't it awful how an illness like this can so trap a person," he replied.

Frank appeared to be much calmer in himself during the following weeks. Although his physical symptoms were no longer a problem and he seemed relatively comfortable and mobile, he opted to base himself in the hospice, going home at the weekends. During this time he talked openly with his family and the ward staff about his situation. One of the other doctors working with Frank recorded the following conversation from this time in his case notes:

Frank said things like, "The cancer is still there . . . I was discussing death with my brother . . . my energy and interests are low . . . how does one know one is dying? . . . are all patients here told they are dying when the time comes?" I replied "no" to this final question and added that his body would tell him when that time was near. "My body is telling me a lot these days," he replied. Our conversation went on like that, it was all centred on death. We then discussed the gap between knowing the "facts" of having terminal cancer and emotionally accepting the reality of these facts. It seemed to me that Frank was *in* that gap and trying to move towards emotional acceptance. The feeling I came away with was sadness. His sadness at knowing "the end was near." Later, chatting with Frank's brother, I felt he was trying to cheer Frank up and to help him to get over this sadness. I suggested to him that it might be more helpful to stay with Frank and to share the sadness now.

Over the following two weeks Frank became gradually but noticeably weaker. He remained settled and apparently content in himself. All those involved in his care felt that his death was very close. That Sunday morning he announced to the nurse helping him to bathe that he was going to go home for a few hours later that day. He added, "While I'm a bit anxious about how it will go, I really want to make the visit." After a short time at home he became confused and had to be brought back to the hospice earlier than planned. On his return, he was seen by the doctor on duty, who found him to be extremely weak and unwell. He died in the early hours of the following morning.

Frank's sense of "awfulness" was the emotional cost of his using denial as a psychological defense mechanism. Denial works as a psychological protective mechanism by keeping unconscious those aspects of reality which would otherwise be too painful or too frightening to confront consciously: a psychological version

MORTALLY WOUNDED

of "out of sight, out of mind." For most people, denial works successfully and is not so much a phase an individual passes through as an inner shield which that individual slips behind from time to time when in need of respite from the stresses of their situation. For some, however, denial does not work very well: the fear and anxiety induced by the events which generated the denial "leak" out, either through physical symptoms, as in Sean's uncontrollable pain, or, as seen here with Frank, through emotional symptoms. In denying the reality of his approaching death, Frank was also cutting himself off from the inner unknown, the dark and meaningful depths of soul. While this kept him in the safety and familiarity of his surface mind, it also resulted in feelings of pointlessness and hopelessness.

Soul pain and clinical depression have much in common. The characteristic struggle to find a way out of soul pain, as it appeared in Frank's story, has many features similar to those of acute agitated depression, while soul pain that has been present over a prolonged period of time can come to look like an apathetic depression, where such individuals may have feelings of alienation, dryness, and meaninglessness as they progressively withdraw from life and living. Whereas Frank's family doctor had diagnosed his distress as an episode of depression, I saw it as soul pain. Given the fact that depression and soul pain can manifest in very similar ways, how can we know if we are dealing with a biological problem causing secondary emotional and psychological effects, with a phenomenon that is primarily psychospiritual in its origins, or perhaps a combination of both in the one individual? I do not know the answer to this. The real importance of what language we use to describe a person's experience, however, is that it affects how we view that experience, which in turn influences how we act in response to it. My difficulty with labeling Frank's sense of awfulness simply as an episode of acute depression, and *only* prescribing antidepressant medication by way of response, was that this response seemed to miss the full existential dimensions of his suffering and ultimately to devalue what he was living. In addition, this diagnosis, by reinforcing Frank's view of himself as the powerless "victim" and his caregivers as the powerful "heroes," was exacerbating rather than easing the very problem it was attempting to resolve.

It is not that I am happy the antidepressants prescribed for Frank did not work while my interventions did, so proving me "right" and his family doctor "wrong." I have no difficulty in accepting that the psychological and spiritual event that is soul pain may be associated with biological changes and would agree that psychologically active medication, including antidepressants, may, in some cases, have a helpful role to play. However, such a treatment is only one small part of what needs to be a far more holistic response to the phenomenon of soul pain. Put another way, to only have seen what Frank was experiencing as depression and to have responded only with antidepressants would have been a purely superficial response to the surface features of soul pain. What was needed was a way of responding that also addressed the deeper aspects of what he was living. Calling Frank's suffering soul pain meant acknowledging that more than biomedical skills and expertise were needed here.

Frank's sharing his thoughts of suicide during that early meeting allows us to consider the question of what someone who is in soul pain and already close to death is really asking for when they say that they wish their life was over, when they share with us their feeling that they want to end their own life, or when they ask us directly for help to die. I believe that many times the plea to "Put me out of my suffering, I can't go on like this," could read, "Get me out of my suffering, I need help, this is unbearable." What may drive an individual to consider suicide or euthanasia in terminal illness is uncontrolled and overwhelming physical or emotional pain, or the expectation that such horrors await them in the future. The reality is that it is neither necessary to be killed nor to kill the person to kill the pain. What is needed here is skilled and effective palliative care which can free such individuals from their unbearable suffering and offer them a new lease on life. However, situations may arise where, despite successful palliation of symptoms (and medical attempts to treat a suspected clinical depression, as in Frank's case), an individual persists in expressing a longing for death or in asking for help to die, perhaps adding that life has now lost all meaning.

For someone working purely from the medical model and at the surface level of reality such situations are intolerable and, as discussed earlier, trigger the caregiver's own ego survival reactions. Caregivers may then give someone like Frank bigger and bigger doses of sedative medications with the intention of relieving his suffering, and ultimately achieve this by having the patient asleep most, if not all, the time. While agreeing that on occasions this line of treatment is necessary, I wish to return to the patient's words "Help me to die" and to suggest that there is another way of understanding and responding to this plea.

If we work *only* at a surface level and from within the medical model, we will see this request in literal terms and, totally identified with our now frightened and frustrated heroic mode, may be in danger of coming to the mistaken conclusion that the only way to end that person's suffering (and ours) is by killing the person. This logic is flawed. It is also dangerous, with the danger, as Hillman reminds us, lying "not in the death fantasy, but in its literalism." In terms of soul pain, someone who is asking for help to die is crying out for depth, pleading for help to cross over from the surface, where they are trapped and suffering, to the release of the unknown deep. By hearing an individual's request in this way and by responding appropriately, we can help that person to die *metaphorically*. We can, in other words, help that person to die without killing them.

This was how I saw Frank's suicidal thoughts and his longing for death: as both the desperate cry of someone struggling to find a way out of suffering and an indication of where that release might be found—in the metaphorical death involved in his making a descent to the underworld of soul. The imagework Frank undertook, in the setting of the palliative care he was already receiving, is what enabled that descent to occur.

Initially Frank had some difficulty with the imagery, and I wondered if he was someone who simply could not work in this way, such as I have occasionally, although rarely, encountered. If this had been the case, we as a team would have considered another depth skill such as bodywork, music therapy, or some form of meditation which might have suited him better. As it turned out, his difficulty was not with imagery per se, but with the leap straight into evocative and spontaneous imagery. Perhaps the loss of control involved in this particular way of working with imagery was too daunting for him at that point. I, therefore, initially used a guided imagery approach, which may have felt safer to him, and in this way led him to the place where he had to make a choice whether or not to trust his own imagination. This began as he allowed the emergence of an image of a wise person who was waiting for him and was confirmed at the point of his deciding whether or not to go into the cottage and enter into dialogue with this wise person.

This was an important moment. An individual may meet the world of images and return untouched and unchanged. While the first step has to do with entering into the image world, the second and more important step has to do with *one's attitude to that world while there.* If the individual enters to mock or to plunder, nothing happens and the images encountered there remain, at best, an interesting illusion. If, on the other hand, that individual enters like Frank, as witness and novice and with a willingness to be there as apprentice, the images are experienced as a living reality, and anything may happen.

As Frank chose to trust the image world of soul, his descent

accelerated. The details of this part of the imagework are interesting. The little cottage was in the west, where the sun dies and
where the entrance to the underworld of Hades is said to be
located, and the wise person who answered his call came in the
form of a dead friend, Joe. Frank, who had spoken of suicide, had
indeed descended to death's dark kingdom. This is where he was
able to voice his deepest need and could open himself to receiving the understanding of his friend's silent reassurance.

The way I helped Frank to work with the dream encounter
with the Russians which he had a few nights later is a variation
of spontaneous or evocative imagework. I especially value working with an individual's own dream images, as I know that these
are fine-tuned by that individual's own unconscious for that
particular situation at that particular time. The aim of this type
of dream work is not dream interpretation, as this can all too easily lead to dream dissection and dream destruction. This would be
the heroic approach to dreams which, like Hercules when he
descended to Hades, leaves murdered animals, wounded gods,
and dead dreams in its wake. What is needed is an approach to
dreams which Hillman calls "dream conservation," the golden
rule of which is to approach and work with the dream in ways
that "keep the dream alive." The underlying thesis of this form
of dream work is that there is an innate, dynamic healing
wisdom in the dream images, something that can be experienced rather than intellectually known by a person willing to
trust the dream, allowing it to act as it desires and to lead where
it will.

The content of Frank's dream shows that the various parts of
the Chiron myth are not "stages" that a dying individual moves
through sequentially in an orderly progression. While the
choice and descent of the preceding imagework session were
undoubtedly genuine, the dream illustrated the continuing
struggle which was simultaneously active in other parts of his
psyche. Frank's very survival seemed to depend on his dream

visitors' remaining unidentified and unnamed, which he in turn related to his wish that details of his prognosis remain uncertain. When he reentered this dream sequence, however, and his visitors asked him what it was he most needed from them, he seemed to move beyond this fear to a desire that he be believed. Their words "We believe you, we believe you and we will not forget you" evidently touched him very deeply; he spoke of feeling "like it was God talking."

When Frank asked me for more information about his condition and likely prognosis, it was evident that he was responding to something in himself other than the voice that warned that such information would mean he would be "trapped forever." It seemed as if the dream and the subsequent work he did with it helped him to face the very source of his fear, recognizing, paradoxically, that this might well be the way out of the prison he was already in. Receiving this information brought a shift in how he saw his situation. This was apparent in his words: "Isn't it awful how an illness like this can so trap a person." The sense of "awfulness" and of being "trapped" were still there but they no longer had the same tyrannical power. These feelings were now just one part of a much bigger picture and seemed to echo Sean's words: "The pain is still there but I can live with it now." I remember feeling around this time that something had also changed between Frank and me. We were now relating on very much more equal terms than previously.

A potential problem in telling Frank's story, and others in this section of the book, is that they may read as if everything was turmoil and strife until the magic wand of imagework was waved, when all became happy ever after. The reality here, as in the other stories, was not like that. This is not to say that what I call the movement into depth did not make a difference. However, the inner shift that led to the qualitative change in Frank himself, as was the case for Sean and Dara, was made possible because the essential environment for such a change to occur had already been created by the palliative care these individuals were receiving. This change was something subtle and intangible and could easily have been missed by the casual onlooker. To family and staff who knew him well, however, the difference was evident and was something felt viscerally. As a caregiver I no longer had that sense of desperation when I was with Frank, the feeling that "I must do something to help" coupled with panic and impotence at my inability to do so. Nothing was different, and yet everything had changed.

That Frank continued to struggle emotionally is apparent from his conversation with the other ward doctor a couple of weeks later. As she so accurately put it, there was an enormous gap between his knowledge of the facts and his emotional acceptance of those facts. Frank was in that very gap, touching the emotional acceptance and then flitting back again, like a moth circling a flame. Her counsel to his brother is pertinent. He was finding it unbearably painful to hear Frank talk of his impending death. His desire to ease the pain led him to attempt to jolly Frank along to a more comfortable place for them both. This was not what Frank needed. Acceptance is not something an individual can choose at will. It is not like some light switch that can at will be flicked on or off. Deep emotional acceptance is like the settling of a cloud of silt in a troubled pool. With time the silt rests on the bottom and the water is clear. And so the doctor's advice to the brother is good advice: "Don't do too much. Just be there. Time will do the rest."

"Well, I'm Not a Medieval Mystic": Bairbre's Story

I met Bairbre for the first time as she lay struggling for breath in her single hospital room. It was early December. I had been asked to see her to try to help improve the extreme shortness of breath which was making her life a misery. She had been read-mitted to the hospital two weeks previously when an X ray showed that malignant melanoma had now spread to the lymph nodes in the center of her chest and was beginning to block her airways. The radiotherapist had given her a course of treatment to try to relieve this, but, as yet, this had not improved her breathlessness. She had great difficulty speaking at this stage, because of having to breathe so quickly and because talking triggered off spasms of coughing, during which she nearly choked on thick, sticky phlegm.

My first impressions were of an extremely ill, distressed middle-aged woman. The curtains were drawn in her room and the light was dim. Her husband, Joe, was sitting by her bedside. As I sat down at the other side of the bed, I was conscious of the noises in the room: Bairbre's labored breathing and the hissing of oxygen through the plastic nasal prongs she wore. She was lying propped up by lots of pillows, with her right arm, swollen because of pressure from lymph nodes in her neck, resting on a small cushion across her lap.

"I hope you can help me," she sighed as she closed her eyes in exhaustion. Then Joe began to tell the story of Bairbre's long struggle with illness. From time to time she opened her eyes and came into the conversation, correcting or adding certain details.

As Joe finished, Bairbre said, "Three years ago I was told I was unlikely to be alive in twelve months' time. Since then I've had two and a half great years. This has been coming on for the past six months. It feels different this time. I have struggled long enough." I asked if she felt worried or frightened when she looked toward the future. "I'm not frightened of death," she replied, "but I'm terrified of what I might have to go through between now and then. I just don't want it to go on like this."

When I visited Bairbre two days later, the new medication had begun to take effect. Her breathing was easier and she was no longer having the spasms of coughing. She looked very much more at ease. I noticed that the nasal prongs were still in place even though the oxygen, now no longer needed, had been switched off. She told me about herself and her family. Although she came from Dublin, where many of her original family including her mother still lived, her home was in Kerry, where she had worked as a teacher in a school where Joe was headmaster. They had three children, the elder two at the university in Dublin, the youngest son completing his final year of school in Kerry. We spoke about where she would like to spend Christmas. If she had been well enough she would have liked to make the journey home to Kerry, but memories of her recent terrifying breathlessness were obviously still with her, and she felt nervous at the prospect. Joe then arrived and joined in the discussion. This concluded in their deciding that Bairbre would base herself in the hospital in Dublin over Christmas, going out to visit family and friends as much as she was able to.

I next saw Bairbre early in the new year, on returning from the holidays. She had remained comfortable over Christmas, and although she had not been well enough to leave the hospital, she had obviously been surrounded by love and laughter. The memories of those days brought tears to her eyes. "Each moment was all the more wonderful knowing I wouldn't see another Christmas. It's the pain of letting go of the people I love.

I don't want to." She then turned to me and asked, "Should I be reading Kübler-Ross? I've a feeling of being a complete novice in all this . . . what can I do to prepare myself for what's ahead?" I suggested that it might not be so much about more information at this point as about working with and looking at her experience in a different way. I spoke about the potential value of imagework and how her imagination could become a bridge to her own deep inner wisdom. Bairbre was obviously curious at the sound of this and agreed to go ahead with a first imagework session there and then.

I asked Bairbre to close her eyes and to bring her attention, sequentially and slowly, to whatever she was experiencing at that moment in her body, her feelings, and her mind. I then suggested that she come back to that part of herself that noticed all this, the aware part of herself that was at one with and more than these other parts of herself, and to rest in this place.

"And now, Bairbre, imagine yourself standing on a grassy hill," I said. "It's a summer's evening and the sun is beginning to set in a clear sky. It's still warm. There is just a very faint breeze, which you feel on your face and in your hair. As you look around you can see, in the middle distance, a river. It's wide and obviously deep. Its surface is still and smooth, and the black waters hardly appear to be moving. It's coming from hills to one side, and you can see it meandering its way to the sea on the far distant western horizon. You look down the hill. You notice that between you and the river is a large green field. You begin to descend through the tall grass toward the river. You know that waiting for you on the bank of the river is someone who knows you and cares deeply about you. You are now getting closer to the river. You can see the person standing there. It may be someone you know well, or it may be someone who is unfamiliar to you. You also know that this is someone wise, someone who knows the river and who will be your guide on the next stage of your journey. As you approach this person, he or she greets you and points toward a little wooden rowboat tied at the riverbank nearby. This person is offering to take you in the boat. This is a choice you have to make. Whether or not you will trust this person, whether or not you will get into the boat." At this point I paused and watched Bairbre. She looked as if deeply asleep. If she had been, I would have left it there. I asked, "Is your choice to get into the little boat with this wise person?" Without moving or opening her eyes, she mumbled, faintly but clearly, "Yes."

I continued, "Your guide gets into the boat before you. He or she is sitting on the middle seat and indicates to you to sit in the rear of the boat. You do, and your guide pulls the rope into the boat and, using an oar, pushes the little boat out toward the center of the enormous river. You know that you are with someone who cares deeply about you. You know that you are with someone who knows about the boat and who understands the river. You do not know where this will bring you to, but you do know that you are with someone who knows the way there. You have done all you can. At this stage you can choose to trust yourself to this guide and to trust yourself to the river. Let your guide lead the way. Let the river carry you. Allow yourself to be carried, to be held by this deep and silent river that is flowing into the next stage of your journey. Be aware, notice, experience how this feels. Allow this experience. Allow yourself to be carried." I waited a minute or so and then said, "Bairbre, if you are awake, begin to come back to the here and now, and when you are ready, open your eyes so we can talk about this." As the minutes passed it was evident that she was asleep. I said good-bye and left the room, and asked the nursing staff to ensure that she was not interrupted by visitors for the next hour or so.

It was Thursday, two days after that first imagework session, that I next visited Bairbre. She was physically very comfortable. In the frame of her mountain of pillows she looked tired and very frail. She also appeared to be calm and at peace, and said that this was how she had been feeling over the past couple of days. She said that she found the imagework session "amazing" and that it was difficult for her to believe that something so simple could have such powerful effects.

Bairbre remained like this over the weekend, but the following Monday morning she awoke to an attack of breathlessness and panic. She was very frightened and agitated and called out that she wanted to die. She accepted the suggestion of the medical and nursing staff to have some sedative medication, following which she went to sleep. When she awoke the panic had passed, but she said that she was feeling "desperate." I heard this from Joe when I arrived on the ward the following day. He described what Bairbre had gone through as "mental anguish" and said that he had never seen her like this before. It had obviously been horrendous for him to witness her like this and be utterly incapable of bringing comfort to her. Joe and I went in to see Bairbre together.

Bairbre, drowsy but calm, greeted me with the words, "I can't see any point in going on like this. I have said all my good-byes. I have done all I can do. I want it all to be over now." She described how she felt it was not in her control to change how it was, try as she might. "This is a new experience for me. I have never felt like this before. And I feel completely alone in it. Like that film of the boy who was born with no immune system and had to live in a glass bubble—I seem to be looking out at everyone; they're out there, I'm in here and between us is this invisible barrier."

I struggled to find words to reply. "Maybe," I began, "maybe it's not about 'doing' at the moment. All life long we react to problems and pain by doing something, by finding something to fix it and make it better. Maybe the pain you are experiencing at present can't be fixed in this way. Perhaps the intensity of this pain might ease if you could in some way allow it and accept that this time you don't have the answer. It may be that if you can give this experience space, unpleasant as it is, *it* may carry you through to another place." Bairbre looked straight ahead as I spoke. As I finished, she looked into my eyes. I found it hard to understand her expression. I thought I saw tiredness and hopelessness, and irritation.

I determined to try again. "Bairbre, do you remember the imagework we did together almost a week ago?"

"Yes," she replied, "that was wonderful, what you did for me there. It seems a million miles away at the moment. But that was imaginary, this is real."

"Yes, it was imaginary but it was not an illusion," I said. "The imaginary landscape I led you through is really your own inner landscape. That river with its quiet power is there, way down in the depths of yourself. I didn't do anything for you, other than help you to access that place in yourself. It's yours and it's there today also, it's just that you are not in contact with it. Meister Eckhart, a medieval mystic, wrote that God is like a great underground river. The underground river is there, Bairbre, way down inside you. Even if you can't feel it, you can choose to trust that it is there."

Bairbre turned to face me again. This time her anger was more apparent. "Well, that is not where I am. I am not some medieval mystic. I bet you he wasn't dying when he wrote those words."

I realized then that I was desperately trying to do the impossible, to fix her pain with my words. Whereas I had been leaning toward her, I now sat back. I didn't know what to say. I felt confused.

Slowly lifting her finger, Bairbre pointed at the gap in the wooden dado rail on the wall facing her bed. "I am there," she said, pointing to where the wooden rail ended at one side of the gap. "I would like to be there," she added, pointing to where the rail began again at the other side of the gap, "but I'm not."

"I'm sorry, Bairbre," I said. "You're right. It is easy for me to say these things. I'm not in your situation. I don't know how it is, what it feels like. What seems important right now is that you stay with how you are and how you feel."

I was about to leave, but I hesitated and said, "It doesn't seem to be about words, Bairbre, but, perhaps, if you would like, we could end this meeting with some imagework?" She replied that she would like that. Joe said that he would wait outside. I then took Bairbre through an imaginary sequence identical to that before. The only difference was that this time, when she met with the wise guide at the edge of the river, I suggested that she might like to talk for a while to this person. "Tell him or her exactly how you feel at this moment, what you want, what you need, and notice what response this person makes to you." As I finished I noticed that Bairbre had fallen asleep. I left her sleeping and went outside to talk to Joe.

I next visited Bairbre the following afternoon. She seemed relaxed and happy in a quiet sort of way. I asked her about yesterday's exercise. "I didn't find it quite so easy as the previous one," she said. "When I came to the side of the river, I couldn't see the wise person's face, yet I knew it was my father. I hadn't the easiest of relationships with him. The choice I seemed to be faced with at that point was whether or not I could believe that he accepted me as I was. I did and got into the boat."

I called again the following day. "I'm beautiful today," Bairbre said. "This is exactly how I hoped I would be . . . no discomfort . . . at peace . . . not frightened." Until now there had always been one of her family present when I had visited. This is how she had wanted it, as she said it made her feel secure and less fearful. It seemed significant, therefore, that on this occasion she was alone in her room.

Four days after this, Bairbre had what the nursing staff described as "another panic attack." She had become very fearful and agitated and felt as though she could not catch her breath. Some of her family were with her at the time, and they tried unsuccessfully to comfort her. They then called in one of the nurses who, having also failed in her attempts to calm Bairbre, offered her an injection to help her to relax. Bairbre accepted; she was given a tranquilizing injection and soon settled into a deep sleep.

I visited Bairbre later that afternoon. She was still asleep, but wakened when I called her name. "I felt terrified," she mumbled drowsily, "I don't know what of. I feel such a failure. I'm not coping and . . . I'm letting you down." I was shocked by her final comments but realized they were at least partially true. When the nurses had told me of her panic attack, my immediate feelings had been of disappointment. I now recognized that this disappointment was not just for Bairbre's sake, it was also because her attack did not fit into "my plans" for how her dying should be.

I did not know what to say in response to this. I was also conscious of the fact that I was in a hurry and would have to leave her shortly. "Bairbre, it's all right to have those feelings. I'm not saying it's easy or pleasant. It's not. It's hard and it's horrible. It's part of what you are going through, and it's part of your humanity. It doesn't mean you're not coping. It means you're human. And you're not letting me down. I am sorry if I've made you feel this way. It's not about being fearless in the face of death. It's about learning to live with your fear, and allowing yourself to receive whatever help you need from others to do so. Today that meant allowing yourself to receive some medication. If this was happening to someone close to you, someone you loved dearly, would you expect them to get through an experience like this without fear or without accepting whatever help was on offer? Perhaps there is also a part of you that is judging your performance in this, a part that sets impossibly high standards and speaks with a critical voice? Perhaps you need to tell this part of yourself to be quiet. While Bairbre the fifty-year-old woman is lying there in the bed, lying beside her is Bairbre the little girl, who doesn't like the dark. She needs all the holding she can get, and she needs to be allowed to be frightened." She listened to all this, heavy-eyed but attentive. Before leaving we agreed to add a small dose of tranquilizer to her other regular medications.

That night Bairbre had a bad nosebleed. She had by then become jaundiced, which had made her more prone to hemorrhage, and at one point the bleeding was so profuse that the night nurse thought she was going to die and called her family in. She did not die, and medication she was given at the time of the bleed had an amnesiac effect, so that she remembered little when she awoke the following morning. I visited her that afternoon. Joe was with her at the time. She looked pale and weak, but was calm and alert. When I asked her how she was feeling, Bairbre replied, "Nostalgic." As I left her room I bumped into her mother, who was on her way in. She walked up the corridor with me, and I told her how I had found Bairbre and of her description of how she was feeling. She drew a distinction between the "quiet nostalgia" that was now there, and the painful emotions of grief that had been there up to recently. As I left the hospital the word "winsome" came to mind, but I was unclear whose feelings this word described.

Two days went by before I saw Bairbre again. These had passed uneventfully for her, and the nurses told me that she had been calm and comfortable. When I went in, I found her enfolded in pillows, looking relaxed but weary. Indeed, she was so tired that there was, for the first time, no emotion in her face, and it seemed to take great effort for her to turn her head and speak. Her sister Louise, her great friend and ally, was sitting at the other side of the bed. Holding Bairbre's hand she recapped the conversation they had just been having. "I was telling her she can let go now," she said. "She has given everyone so much love, she has done all she wanted and needed to do. Yesterday she said to me that she wished that it was all over. I've been telling her that it is fine to feel this way, and I've been encouraging her to take the odd 'gin and tonic' of additional medication if she needs a few hours out of the limelight."

As Louise finished speaking, Bairbre, who had been watching her sister, turned slowly in my direction. "Why not?" I agreed. "A woman in labor is doing the work herself, but the help of a wise midwife can occasionally come in handy. It won't be long now, Bairbre." She sighed as she closed her eyes. "Good-bye for now," I said. She opened her eyes and said, "God bless." "God bless you too," I replied. As I left I felt the end was very near. I also remember feeling that it was time for me to bow out of the picture. It was as if I had gone along the road with Bairbre as far as I could go. It was now time for me to let her go ahead on her own. Later that day Bairbre slipped into a coma. Her family stayed with her through the night. She died in the early hours of the following morning.

When I first met Bairbre I saw her as a confident woman who appeared to be coping remarkably well in very difficult circumstances. Here was someone who knew she was going to die shortly and was determined to use her remaining time to do everything possible to prepare herself and her family for what lay ahead.

My initial contract with Bairbre was, in the terms I have been using, to work with her as doctor/hero at the surface level of her distress. This was the expectation of the medical colleague who had asked for my help, of her family, and of Bairbre herself. Through the palliative treatments I started I was able to meet most of these expectations. For the majority of people I work with my contribution to their care would have ended there. While I would then continue to visit them from time to time to ensure that they remained physically comfortable and to listen and talk to them or their family about their concerns or worries, I would not normally intervene beyond this surface level, trusting that good palliative care and time would do this for them. Bairbre, however, was saying that she wanted more than this.

As she was an academic and an intellectual, Bairbre interpreted her feelings of wanting to look at what she was living more fully as a need for information and rational understanding of the process of dying. She expressed this as a question at the end of our third meeting about what literature she should read to prepare and educate herself for whatever lay ahead. In her desire to know more about dying and death I sensed a longing for depth and felt that she was asking for help in this. In suggesting imagework to her, I hoped that it might enable her to move, if she so wished, from her surface mind where reason alone was unable to give her what she was seeking, into the way of descent, where what she was living would be experienced less as ideas and more as emotion and intuition.

The river exercise I did with Bairbre is a predominantly guided imagework. The advantage of guided imagework here was that it allowed me to lead Bairbre in a particular direction in a way that would feel safe to someone doing imagework for the first time. In terms of the Chiron myth, the direction I wanted to lead her in was toward the lower half of her experience and the underworld of her imagination. In terms of the psychological model, this meant a move into her deep mind and toward the underground river of her deep center or essential self. Built into this exercise were elements which called on her creative imagination and confronted her with a crucial choice which only she could make. It was up to her to imagine the wise guide who waited for her on the banks of the river and to decide whether or not to entrust herself to this guide and to step into the next part of her journey.

Bairbre's own word to describe that initial imagework session was "amazing." She was surprised by how powerful such an apparently simple technique could be and felt calm and peaceful in the days that followed. Her description is similar to that of many others who experience the effects of active imagination at this stage of their lives. It is as if the depths are ready and waiting for that individual to take even one small step in their direction. Bairbre's choice to get into the boat with her wise guide was a deliberate choice to place her trust in depth. Her subsequent sense of calm and peace was the soulful experience of one being held by the deep or essential self.

What Bairbre experienced, as a result of imagework and the other psychological work she did on her own and with others in her final weeks, is similar to what is seen as a much more gradual process, often over a period of years, in an individual undergoing psychoanalytic psychotherapy. Here, in a process of inner healing sometimes called "individuation," a person slowly, and often painfully, moves from a surface-mind and ego-based existence to a deep-mind and self-based existence. This would seem to confirm the observation of depth psychologist Edward Edinger that for those close to death, the individuation process can be accelerated and that there is "an urgency on the part of the unconscious to convey awareness of a metaphysical reality, as if such an awareness were important to have before one's physical death." To say that this process can somehow be accelerated or telescoped in those close to death is not, however, to imply that it is either simple or straightforward. Rather, it is a matter of that individual's progressing with the seemingly circular movements of a spiral, where each curve and twist takes in more and more of who that person really is.

As if to emphasize this point, less than a week after that initial and positive imagework session, Bairbre had a panic attack which left her very much more frightened and upset than she had been before. It seemed to be the polar opposite to the sense of well-being she experienced in the previous days and to confirm her worst fears of what dying might be like. What had happened? One explanation is that the letting go to depth at the center of the imagework session was the "final straw" from the ego's point of view. The eruption into consciousness of undiluted terror and panic may, therefore, have been the desperate expression of her increasingly threatened ego rebelling against its loss of control. While Bairbre had dealt with her dying intellectually and had experienced certain feelings as part of her grieving, there were other feelings such as anger, fear of the unknown, and hopelessness which had, until then, been deeply buried and split off from her conscious awareness.

This episode also revealed something about the limitations in how I had been working with Bairbre. In my desire for her to experience the healing power of depth, I had been hasty and had failed really to allow her space for feelings. This was indicative of both my impatience and my own problem with "difficult" emotions and, in the medium term, had the opposite effect to what I had wanted for her. Indeed, it added a new dimension to her distress by making her feel that she was "failing" herself, and me, in reacting in such an utterly human way.

A consequence of moving from the hero-victim roles of the medical model into the kind of wounded healer relationship which becomes operative when working in this deep, imaginative way is that the individuals in such a relationship are now primarily present to each other as two human beings, both standing on the edge of the known and searching together for a path forward. This is not without risks. One of the advantages of the old hierarchical relationship was that professional boundaries were as sharp as they were rigid. It was as clear who was the patient and who was the doctor as it was clear who had the problem and who had the answer. In the wounded healer relationship this may not be so evident. In Bairbre's story a blurring of boundaries became evident at this point, as her story and mine began to merge. Confirmation that this was so came in her apology for failing me by having this panic attack, and in my feelings, despite my verbal protestations to the contrary, that somehow she had. Such a situation was potentially dangerous and could have had harmful results. Shortly afterward, however, I was able to discuss this in my ongoing psychotherapy supervision, which helped me to recognize what was happening and to redefine the boundaries between Bairbre's experience and my own. This enabled me to approach future meetings with more clarity and to give Bairbre more psychological space in these encounters.

As Bairbre's panic triggered mine, my verbal efforts to comfort her became a crude attempt to ease the pain, for both our sakes. Her reply to me as I quoted Meister Eckhart's words was the slap in the face I needed. I had begun to engage in what I consider one of the worst professional crimes in this area of work: deathbed evangelization. I was offering Bairbre "my" answers to questions which only she could begin to address. Her retort, "Well, I'm not a medieval mystic," brought me from the dizzy heights of fine theory to a confrontation with a flesh-and-blood woman of feeling.

Perhaps the best thing I could have done at this point would have been to apologize and leave. I knew that more words were not the answer, and yet I was reluctant to walk away from a situation as unfinished as this. Whose pain was I responding to? To say that I was acting to ease the hurt of my own bruised and frustrated ego is at least partially true. I also believed that beneath Bairbre's suffering and beyond any words we might share, there was, within her, a place of deep inner comfort. I wanted to help her to move toward this place, a move she was evidently unable to make on her own. That she too wanted this was apparent in her enthusiastic agreement to my suggestion of ending this meeting with a further imagework session. Despite my reservations at the time, her comment at our next meeting—"I am beautiful"—reassured me that this intervention had been appropriate.

Even though, a few days later, Bairbre had yet another panic attack, this return to terrifying struggle did not belie the reality of her inner descent. Rather it demonstrated, yet again, how movement through the different parts of the Chiron process is neither linear nor absolute. A person may need to make the descent not once and for all, but on a number of occasions. The grip of the old ego-dominated life view is tenacious and especially likely to reassert itself when it feels its dominion threatened by approaching death or the type of death-rehearsal which the imagework entails. This is particularly likely to happen when there are still tasks to attend to at a surface level. In Bairbre's case these included her having to experience particular emotions which she had previously repressed, and completing the task of saying her good-byes to those she loved.

My ongoing psychotherapy supervision enabled me to have a different attitude to Bairbre's fear in the later stages of our working together. While previously her own sense of failure had fed into my sense of disappointment, I now found that I was able to reassure her that it was not about dying without fear, but about each of us finding our own way of living with the fear and other painful emotions that are an inevitable part of our dying. For Bairbre, this included her agreeing to having occasional tranquilizing medication if she felt she needed it. Her ability to accept this type of help represented a softening in her and my expectations, which had previously been impossibly high, and a deeper acceptance of her humanity.

The day after her big nosebleed, Bairbre had become noticeably weaker but seemed to be at peace. Her own word to describe how she felt at that time—"nostalgic"—was interesting. When her husband had suggested that this might mean that she was missing her home in Kerry, it was obvious from Bairbre's reaction that this was not all she was saying. Her mother's interpretation seemed to add the missing piece. She said that perhaps her daughter was not just speaking of feelings of grief for what she was leaving behind, but was also describing a yearning for more of what she was already beginning to experience, and what she sensed lay ahead.

*   *   *

(Just over a year after Bairbre's death, I received a letter from her sister, Louise. I include the following passage from this letter with her permission. "Bairbre's illness, dying and death were among the most important things that have ever happened to me and although I still grieve, I look back on the last few months of her life as being a time of enormous growth for both of us. She told me that I had given her permission to die and I know that I was able to help her to die well, as she wanted to. She in her turn gave me the incredible experience of soul to soul communication at a level I will always treasure.")

"It's Not All Right":
Anne's Story

From what I had heard about Anne, I was expecting to meet someone very ill. Instead, when I walked into the dayroom off the oncology ward, I was surprised to find a beautiful young woman who looked fit and well. As we sat, she began to tell me that she had been attending oncology daycare earlier that afternoon. At her last visit, a week previously, she had been told that despite the radiotherapy and chemotherapy she had had following surgery for breast cancer some twelve months before, the cancer had recurred and was now involving both her lungs, her liver, and her bones. She had been offered further chemotherapy and had taken the week to think about this. Since her oncologist could not guarantee a response to this treatment, and because the previous chemotherapy had caused a lot of side effects, Anne had decided not to go ahead with more active treatment. "What's important for me now is the quality of whatever time I have left," she said. "Yes, I'm determined to have as much time as possible—there is so much I want to do, for myself and for my children—and I want that time to be as good as possible. I'm interested in looking into some of the complementary approaches, like visualization and massage, and I'm hoping that the palliative care service might also be able to help me."

I told Anne what the palliative care approach might have to offer her, emphasizing that the focus of this approach was on the quality of her living. I explained that while we worked within the orthodox medical system, we were also open to complementary approaches and that I had a particular interest in working with visualization. I added that I would be very happy to work in this way with her in the future, if she would like this. I then asked her if there were any particular problem areas where I might be able to help. Anne replied that she had few physical problems, and that apart from occasionally feeling breathless when she rushed or exerted herself, she would not have known there was anything wrong with her. She said that she was continuing her work in business administration and added that "being a single parent is like another full-time job."

Anne told me that she and her husband had separated a couple of years previously. It was obvious that although she had gone through this process some time before, the unresolved pain of it all was still very raw. She expressed concern for how this had affected her three boys, saying that they had found that time very traumatic and needed the support of counseling to help them through. She said that she wanted to find whatever help she could for them and begin to make plans for their futures. We ended that first meeting by discussing how, if her family doctor agreed, I could ask the palliative home care team to visit her, and I explained how they would advise her on what to do if any physical problems arose and perhaps, by involving the team social worker, help with some of her family issues.

Three months passed before I next met Anne. She had been readmitted to the hospital because she had become extremely short of breath. An X ray showed that she had accumulated fluid around both her lungs, and the medical team had inserted a tube to drain this fluid, hoping this would improve her breathlessness. When I went into her hospital room I had difficulty in recognizing her as the person I had previously met. She lay asleep, crumpled on her pillows, with an oxygen mask hissing on her face. Her breathing was irregular and rapid. I pulled a chair to her bedside and thought she looked like someone who had already begun to die. When I called her name she opened her eyes and smiled slightly. Between breaths she said that she felt she was dying and that she did not feel afraid. She was obviously exhausted, so I encouraged her to let go to her tiredness and her pillows, and promised that I would come by to see her soon.

Two days afterward I visited Anne again. I had been told that she had improved dramatically once the fluid had been drained from her chest, and that is how I found her. She was sitting up in bed looking thin, tired, and pale, but she was bright and her breathing was easy. She seemed to have little recollection of her admission to the hospital or of how extremely ill she had been. She said she was uncomfortable, as the chest drain tubes were causing pain and she was very constipated. What seemed to be troubling her more, however, was the fact that she was having "nightmares" in which various members of her family had cancer but she did not, which left her feeling "isolated, alone, and unable to communicate." She said that she was hoping for "inner peace," but that this seemed a long way away. I replied that one way of seeing dreams was as messages from our unconscious mind, which is really our friend and an ally. "Even though it might be hard to understand this, perhaps even these unpleasant dreams need to happen to help you move to that place of peace," I suggested. We then discussed what could be done to ease her physical problems, and she said she was happy to try the medication I proposed.

At my next visit, while Anne was physically a lot more comfortable, she said that she still felt very "troubled" in herself. She was worried about her children and had decided that she did not want them to see her like this. "And I'm frightened," she said. "I'm frightened of dying not at peace in myself." I told Anne about imagework, explained how it might help her, and suggested that we could have a session there and then if she would like. She said she would like to give it a try.

I began by asking Anne to close her eyes, helping her to relax. I then invited her to imagine a favorite place, somewhere she knew well, somewhere that held happy memories for her. "I see my family home, where I lived as a child. When I see it I remember the sense of fun, of togetherness, laughter, warmth," Anne said. I then invited her to enter this place if she chose to do so, knowing that inside someone was waiting for her, someone wise and loving, someone who knew her story and who wanted to help her. After a short pause Anne announced, "It's my mother, and she says to me, 'However things are and whatever happens, it will be all right.' "

"And what do you think about that?" I asked.

"I somehow know that this is true, but I want more time, for my boys, for me," Anne replied. "My mother says she wants this for me too and that she would give it to me if she could. She says that if she could, she would swap places with me."

Anne described how devastated her mother had been when the recurrence was diagnosed. She then told me about her youngest brother, Francis, who had been diagnosed as schizophrenic at the age of eighteen, and how he and the family had suffered a lot with this. He had been found dead in the sea when he was just twenty-four. "That also was a tragedy for my mother," she said. Before leaving I told Anne that I believed the work she had just done was valuable and that while the best way of fighting before might have been to struggle against what was happening, perhaps these days the better way was to "go with the flow," to trust her body and even her "downers."

I called back to see Anne a couple of days later. She looked calm, and I noticed that she was slightly flushed. When I inquired how she was feeling, she started to speak of the image-work session and how she had been since then. "Before that I had been feeling dreadful, but that evening I felt different. I noticed a sense of warmth, of heat inside. I asked myself was this due to something that's happened or to some person, but then I realized, in a moment, that this was God, and I had a sense of how much love there is around me, of how loved I am, of God as love. I was filled with the sense that whatever happens, 'all will be well,' and I knew that this was the voice of the part of me that will live on afterward."

Anne then told me that her mother had brought her sons in to see her that evening and how the visit had gone really well. Her youngest boy had told her how much he loved her. I reflected on how she was obviously special to many people, and suggested that this time, despite all the difficulties, could also be a time of healing for her family. She replied that she was still hoping she would "get a couple of months."

Shortly after this, Anne asked one of her doctors whether or not the chest drain procedure had been successful from a medical point of view. Despite being fully aware of her situation, Anne was taken aback when the doctor's reply came in the question, "Have you ever thought about a move to the hospice?" She told me about this incident when I visited later that day. While she initially spoke of her shock and anger at what she saw as the doctor's tactlessness, we later went on to discuss exactly what the hospice might have to offer her and her family. Anne listened carefully to what I had to say about this. By the following morning she had decided that she would like to make the move.

A couple of days later Anne was transferred from the hospital to the hospice. On arrival she was breathless and in some discomfort but seemed happy to be there. Those who met her then for the first time saw her as an extremely ill young woman who, they thought, could not possibly live more than a few days. When asked by the admitting doctor what her hopes from her stay in the hospice were, she said that her chief concern was that her boys be cared for and that she was also hoping to get a little stronger so she could go home for a day.

Anne's first few days in the hospice were unsettled. Her physical condition deteriorated as she became more breathless and developed a cough and a new pain in her arm. She did not want an increase in the medications she was receiving in case this would make her more drowsy, but agreed to try a small dose of nebulized morphine through her oxygen mask, which seemed to help her. On the night of her admission her estranged husband, John, had come in to see her. When the night nurse came on duty, she called in to see Anne and found her upset. The nurse had asked John to leave, but he had argued with her before leaving reluctantly. The following day Anne's sisters were furious and asked that he be prevented from visiting, as his recent visits appeared to have upset Anne so much. The social worker and I spoke to them and agreed that we would talk with John, if this was also Anne's wish. We then both met Anne to discuss this and her wishes for her children. She was obviously relieved at the suggestion that we would see her estranged husband, and also agreed that we would arrange to meet the boys on their own.

A couple of days later the ward sister and I met John. I told him that I believed that Anne's greatest need now was for whatever would enable her to let go. I said that his visits appeared to put Anne in touch with a lot of the unresolved pain around their separation, and that if he really wanted to help her, it would be best to keep his visits short and not to discuss contentious issues or subjects which confronted Anne with decisions she could not make or tasks she could not now undertake. Although he listened and said he could understand what I was saying, he added that he felt there was some sort of family conspiracy to keep him off the scene, even though he was the boys' father and would be caring for them afterward and had much he needed to talk to Anne about.

Shortly after this, the social worker and I met the three boys. We introduced ourselves and said that we wanted to meet them to give them information about how Anne was getting on and to allow them the opportunity to ask any questions they might have. I told them, as gently as I could, that their mother did not have very long to live and explained our plan to ensure that she be as comfortable and well cared for as possible. All three looked lost as I spoke and seemed to receive the news as something they already knew which was simply being confirmed. Despite my trying to put it as gently as possible, I felt my words were hard and unreal. They did not ask any questions at that meeting, and immediately afterward they went to Anne's room and spent some time with her.

The following morning I stopped in to see Anne. She said that she was pleased that both meetings of the previous day had happened and was especially glad to know that the boys' contact with the social worker was one which would continue into the future. She then told me about frightening nightmares which had returned in recent nights which left her troubled and afraid. In one she was trying to make plans for her children's future but was being frustrated in this by someone who was trying to stab her with a large kitchen knife. A detail that she remembered vividly was that the knife blade had icicles on it. I suggested to Anne that it might be useful for us to look at the imagery in this dream together, and she agreed. As she relaxed and focused her awareness on her feelings she described these as "frozen," and later when she brought her awareness to her body she spoke of a "cold feeling" in her right arm. I asked her to amplify this sensation and to allow an image to come. She described a memory that returned as she did this. The winter after her mastectomy (which was right-sided) had been exceptionally cold. The cold had made her right arm ache, which had, in turn, frustrated her as it prevented her from doing all that needed doing. She said that this seemed to echo her current feelings of wanting to be in control but not being so and of having so much she wanted to do but not being able to do it.

"Anne," I said, "might it be helpful to leave words for now and to spend some more time with images?" She nodded her agreement, so I continued, "All right then, close your eyes and let your mind go clear, and begin to imagine a sandy beach on a lakeside. It's a sunny day, and the water in the lake is calm and clear. Beached on the shore you see a small wooden rowboat. I invite you to push the boat into the lake and, if you so choose, to get in, and then slowly and gently begin to row out into the lake. As you row you hear the lapping of the bow-wave as the boat slips through the calm water. You can feel the sun in your face and a faint breeze in your hair. You have, by now, been rowing for some time and you are beginning to approach the opposite shore. As you do, you are aware that there is someone waiting for you there. It is someone wise and loving, someone who cares deeply about you. This person has been waiting for you for a while and has prepared a meal on a beach fire for you. As you approach you turn around, and over your shoulder you can begin to make out who it is."

"It's my brother Francis," Anne said. "I love him . . . we hug . . . I feel like I have died and he is there to welcome me."

"In the situation you're now in, is there anything you would like to say to him?" I asked.

"Francis," she said, "I love you. I haven't felt your presence near me in recent times. I need your help, and I need to hear from you that all will be well. I need comforting now and I need your help when I'm dying."

"And how does he respond to you?" I enquired.

"When Francis became schizophrenic he no longer believed in God. But he believed that this world was a messed up place and that the best was to come. His face says that this is so."

As we spoke afterward about this and about her dreams, I suggested that while there was a part of her that was impotent to change what was happening and that was very worried and frightened, there was another part of her that was not afraid, that still had choices it could make and that somehow knew that all was going to be well. I explained that what seemed to be happening these days was that she was moving between these two places in herself and that her feelings of fear, which were emerging as nightmare images, were an inevitable part of that process.

"It is impossible to move to that place of peace without feeling fear. So perhaps rather than judging or fearing your fear, allow it, give it permission to be there. It's a sign that the process is happening. Perhaps this is the best way of moving through the fear to that other place." Before I left, I asked Anne if she would like me to bring her a copy of a prayer called the "Prayer of Abandonment," by Brother Charles De Foucauld (reproduced on pp. 124–25), which she might find helpful. She said she would, and I came back with it shortly afterward.

I next saw Anne a couple of days later, after the intervening weekend. The nursing staff had told me that things were working out better with her ex-husband. He was visiting less and for shorter periods, and this had eased the tensions with the rest of the family. However, they felt that Anne's overall condition had weakened considerably and that she appeared to be in more physical distress and was frightened at times. I first asked Anne about her physical symptoms, and she told me that she had a new pain in her ribs when she coughed, and about her continuing breathlessness, weakness, and drowsiness. She had developed signs of a chest infection, which explained her new symptoms, and we agreed on a treatment plan including antibiotics, anti-inflammatory gel which the nurses would rub gently on her ribs to ease the pain, a slightly increased strength of the morphine she was already taking for her shortness of breath, and a dose of a cough medication before going to sleep at night.

I then asked how she had been "in herself" over the weekend. She told me of snatches of dreams she remembered from the previous couple of nights. In one she was on a bed with this little boy. He threw her up in the air and they landed on the bed, laughing together. She said the feelings of the dream were of joy and warmth, and this description and her flushed cheeks seemed a marked contrast to the pallor and cold that had been there at the beginning of our last meeting. She also remembered a moment during the previous night when she had been lying there, half awake and half asleep. She said that she had heard what sounded like the feet of lots of "little people" coming into her room. They proceeded to stand silently around her bed, an experience she found more curious than alarming. Anne then looked at me and said, "You know, I feel less frightened of dying these days. Don't get me wrong, it's not that I'm looking forward to it, it's that there is less fear there. I find when I'm on my own and I say the prayer, 'Oh Sacred Heart of Jesus, I place my trust in thee,' it brings me great peace." I replied, "Yes it's going to be all right, Anne. That great deep underground river that is love, that is God, *is* there, and it's going to carry you through." I then asked her if she would like me to pray with her. She said she would. I asked her to rest back into her pillows and close her eyes as she listened to the words of the prayers. I began:

Lord in your mercy hear my prayer
Lord in your mercy hear my prayer
Lord in your mercy hear my prayer
that I may know your prayer,
that I may know your prayer,
that I may know your prayer.

Father, Mother, I abandon myself into your hands,
do with me what you will.
Whatever you may do, I thank you, Lord.
I am ready for all, I accept all,
Let only your will be done in me and in all your creatures,
I ask no more than this, O Lord.
Into your hands, I let go my soul.
I let it go with all of my heart, for I love you, Lord
and so need to give myself, to surrender myself into your
    hands
without reserve and with great confidence
for you are my Father and you are my Mother.

Do not be afraid, Anne, for I have redeemed you.
I have called you by name, you are mine.
Should you pass through the sea, I will be with you;
or through rivers, they will not swallow you up.
Should you walk through fire, you will not be scorched
and the flames will not burn you.
For I am Yahweh, your God, the Holy One of Israel,
    your saviour.
. . . because you are precious in my eyes and I love you,
. . . do not be afraid, for I am with you.

Oh Sacred Heart of Jesus I place my trust in thee,
Oh Sacred Heart of Jesus I place my trust in thee,
Oh Sacred Heart of Jesus I place all my trust in thee.

I had been watching Anne as I said these words. I was struck by her frailty as she lay there, now apparently asleep. With her flushed red cheeks, she looked as if she were on fire.

I arrived on the ward the following morning to the news that Anne had become a lot weaker overnight and was now beginning to die. I went into her room and immediately saw that her condition had worsened. She was asleep and looked as if she was really having to struggle for each breath. She appeared distressed and exhausted. I woke her and asked her if we could give her something extra to make her feel less breathless.

"Will it make me more sleepy?" she asked.

"It may, Anne, but perhaps you need that now. It looks like such a struggle. Would you mind being more sleepy?"

"Yes," she said. "I want to be more awake."

As I left she was again slipping back into an exhausted sleep. I sensed this might be the last time I would see her, so I said, "Good-bye for now, Anne. I hope all goes well." She lifted her head slightly and waved.

When I went outside, her parents and sisters were waiting.

We went into the dayroom off the ward and sat down, and I told them that I felt that time was now very short. I reassured them that although she still had some physical distress, she was not too troubled by this and that I felt she was someone of great inner resources who had prepared, as much as anyone could, for whatever was ahead. There was a feeling of great sadness in the room as I shared this with them. One of Anne's sisters said that when sitting with her in recent days, she had been praying with her, and this seemed to bring her peace. I then mentioned what Anne had said about the "Prayer to the Sacred Heart." Her sister replied, "Yes, we suggested she might say that. Our brother, Francis, used to say it."

In the course of that day Anne slipped in and out of consciousness. Overnight she slept deeply. When I looked in the following morning, her closed eyelids flickered slightly when I called her name. I sat with her for some minutes and repeated some of the prayers from the day before. Later in the morning she awoke and appeared confused and agitated. When I went into her room a nurse was sitting beside a distraught-looking Anne attempting to reassure her. Meanwhile Anne, wide-eyed and kneeling on her bed, was calling out and rummaging through the sheets "looking for my baby." I pulled a chair over so that I was facing Anne, took her hand, and said "Anne, it's okay. We are with you. It's okay. It's going to be all right." At that she stopped her searching for a moment, looked at me as if I were a stranger, and clearly and slowly, with the annoyance of one talking to another who despite repeated attempts could not be made to understand, said, "It's *not* all right." I sat silently for a while. Then I said, "Let go to your body, Anne. Let your body rest now. Let go to the tiredness." She lay back against her pillows and began to settle. Her family were nearby all day, coming in and out of her room. Late in the afternoon she once again became restless and agitated and did not settle with reassurance. I decided that she needed an injection to help her to relax.

Shortly after having this, she went back to sleep. During her final hours Anne remained asleep with her three sons, her parents, her sisters, and her brothers at her bedside. She died early that evening.

Why did the suggestion of a move from the hospital to the hospice make Anne feel so disappointed and fearful? The hospice in Dublin has been in existence for over a hundred years and is well known throughout the city. For many years the words "Hospice for the Dying" were emblazoned over its gateway. Even though this sign has long been removed, and much has been done in recent years to portray it as the "Hospice for the Living," for most Dubliners the words "hospice" and "death" remain synonymous. It seems that although Anne was well informed of her prognosis, the way the hospice was first mentioned to her came as a shock. This suggests that at that stage she was still some way from emotionally accepting that she was close to death. For Anne, therefore, the move to the hospice was itself a kind of dying. The emotion this brought to the surface was the voice of her ego declaring its resistance to such a move.

The first few days of Anne's stay in the hospice were a "busy" time. There was a lot to be done, particularly in terms of her distressing physical symptoms and the unresolved relationship issues. Both Anne and her family needed the full range of multiprofessional expertise that the hospice had to offer. If this expertise had not been available, it is likely that she would have suffered more and might not have been able to do the deep inner preparatory work for her approaching death. Here again, as in other stories throughout this book, it is apparent that palliative care is the essential first stage of depth work.

Without "good enough" palliative care, there is neither the space nor the freedom to dive deep. Unless the surface level of suffering is attended to as skillfully and compassionately as possible, an individual's unresolved physical, emotional, and social distress will remain as chains that bind that person to that dimension of their reality. This was very much the case for Anne, where depth work through imagery, dreams, and prayer was not so much about introducing her to an unfamiliar terrain, in that she was someone who had a rich inner life long before her terminal illness, as about creating an opportunity for her to do what she desired but was neither free nor able to do for herself at the time.

For Anne the move into depth was initially a difficult process. The first imagework session brought her into the roots of her emotional pain, confronting her with feelings of desolation at the prospect of losing her mother, with the acute awareness of her mother's suffering on losing her, and with the still smoldering grief for her brother who had died all those years before. A journey into depth is also a journey into deeper layers of emotion and will often identify specific and sometimes painful issues that need to be faced in the process of dying.

Shortly after the first imagework session Anne became aware of what she called a "warm glow" in the center of her chest and, with this, a sense of being "surrounded by love." I believe that what Anne was describing here was the experience of being enfolded by the deep center or essential self, which many would see as that in us which is continuous with what is infinite and eternal. As she struggled to find words for this experience she spoke of "God" and "love" and that part of herself that would "live on afterward."

Given Anne's personality and her concerns about the unresolved family issues, if she had not received what help she did, she might have struggled on to the end with the impossible task of trying to make it easy and painless for those she loved and was leaving behind. The role depth work played in her case, however, was not simply a matter of helping her to disengage from all that tied her at a surface level so that she could sink unencumbered into depth. This would have been both premature and inappropriate and might have deprived both her, and those she was close to, of something essential to her way of letting go and dying.

It was as though, after years of living on land, in the air, and in the sun, Anne had now begun to relocate to the depths of the ocean. And while the visits to the surface allowed her to rearrange and collect the material she needed for her new home in the depths, the times in depth meant that she brought back to those who waited on the land treasures of love and meaning, gifts which somehow made their pain and sadness a little more bearable. While the episodic journeying into depth allowed her ritually to rehearse the process of dying and brought her great inner consolation, the returning to the surface, the coming up for air, allowed her to bring comfort to her family and say her good-byes. In other words, *all* of what Anne experienced at that time, both on the surface and in the depths, was complementary and valuable to her unique way of living her dying.

Anne's story illustrates that perhaps the best way of looking at the different parts of the Chiron myth is as a constellation of features which may be experienced in any sequence and at any time in the process of dying. Signs of the return had been present for some time in her experience of being loved, in the peace she knew from time to time, and in the consolation that came through her to those around her. Again and again, Anne made the choice to trust, and many times made the descent, while her struggle continued episodically right into the final hours of her life.

The second imagework session is a microcosm of one such working through of the Chiron constellation. At the beginning of that session Anne was in the struggle of physical and emotional distress. In deciding to get into the boat and begin a journey with an unknown destination, she was making the choice to launch out into the deep. She herself articulated the essence of the descent experience when she said, on meeting her (dead) brother, "I feel like I have died and he is there to welcome me."

And finally, the detail that the Sacred Heart prayer, which brought her such comfort, had also been a favorite refrain of her brother Francis, was confirmation that she was in the return.

That second imagework session also helps to put the work of caregivers for dying persons in perspective. While their work is invaluable, we also need to recognize its limitations. Even though the caregivers can walk so far with the dying person, they then have to stop, wait, and let that person move on alone. The appearance at this time of an inner guide, that is, someone from the image world of soul who knows the way forward from lived experience, is a deeply reassuring and significant event. Anne herself recognized Francis as such when she asked him for his help "Now . . . and when I'm dying."

The way I shared prayer with Anne shortly before she died can facilitate a way into depth for some people. It had become evident to me that Anne was a person who was deeply aware of her spirituality and for whom a religious language was an appropriate and effective way to express this inner experience. For another individual, the use of prayer and religious imagery in this way might only have added to his or her sense of alienation. The challenge is to find the appropriate language and approach for that particular individual.

Finally, I will never forget the look in Anne's face, the pause and then the deliberate and irritated tone in her voice as she countered my attempts to calm her shortly before she died with the statement, "It's *not* all right." I have pondered long and hard since then about what Anne was saying. What, exactly, was not all right? These words were spoken by a young woman looking back at me over her shoulder as she stood alone on the threshold of death's dark kingdom. No matter how well intentioned, what was *not* all right was for me to imply in any way that she was overreacting and should not have been making such a fuss, as this failed to acknowledge the enormity of what she was living, and in some way it trivialized her experience. Anne's final words to me do not undermine the central thesis of this book, that good palliative care and preparatory depth work can make a real difference to how we live our dying, but they do put these initiatives in a humbling perspective. They are a reminder that despite all we might say and all we might do, the process of dying includes suffering and painful separations and unfinished business. Death cannot be tamed. Death is unknown. Death is other. Death is death.

> When men die there awaits them what
> they neither expect nor even imagine
> HERACLITUS
> (cited by James Hillman
> in *The Dream and the Underworld*)

Spontaneous Combustion:
James's Story

I had been asked to visit James in the hospital to advise on his palliative care. Before going to see him I read in his case notes that six weeks previously this sixty-seven-year-old man had been brought to the emergency department because of severe chest pain. Investigations he had then showed that he had suffered a heart attack, so he had been admitted immediately to the coronary care unit. While recovering there he had begun to complain of difficulty in swallowing. His doctors had performed further tests and found that he had a massive inoperable cancer of his esophagus. He had subsequently been transferred from coronary care to the general medical ward he was now in.

I went in and introduced myself to James. I explained that I had been asked to visit him to advise on how he could be made more comfortable and to work with him and his family to organize his discharge home from the hospital. As I sat by his bedside and listened to his story, he leaned forward and had to pause every few words to catch his breath. At first he talked of his incapacitating breathlessness and how he was waking during the night gasping for breath. He looked pale and ill and frightened. It was evident that the full diagnosis had not been discussed with him; he told me how he had developed a bad chest infection after his heart attack and that this was all that was now delaying his progress. He said he was very much looking forward to getting home and mentioned his concern about the worry his illness was creating for his wife. He added, finally, that in the past twelve months he had "buried five of his brothers and sisters," and that he, a younger brother, and his sister were the only survivors.

I saw James as an extremely ill man who probably did not have very long to live. Although he had not been told his full diagnosis and prognosis and did not take up my offer to answer any questions he might like to ask, I felt that he probably suspected that things were not going at all well for him. This and his shortness of breath were, as I saw it, making him both anxious and frightened. I suggested that he be started on some medication to ease his breathlessness and a mild tranquilizer at night. I told him that I would come back to see him early the following week, at which stage he might be well enough to make arrangements for his discharge.

When I came back to review James five days later, I was greeted by one of the nurses, who said that she was glad to see me because they were very worried about him. She told me that while both his breathing and disturbed sleep had improved somewhat following my last visit, he had had a very bad night the previous night, caused not by breathlessness but by "the most awful nightmare." Apparently James had been found in the early hours of the morning in a state of agitation, saying that he had had a dream. He had insisted that his two sons be contacted immediately and told to come in to see him. When he failed to "listen to reason," he had been given Valium by the nurse. He eventually settled and went back to sleep.

As I approached his bedside, James appeared to be asleep. I noticed the other men in his ward casting occasional anxious glances in our direction. It struck me that he appeared even more wasted and frail than when I had last seen him just a few days previously. He roused sleepily when I called his name and told him who I was.

"I hear from the nurses that you had a terrible nightmare last night, James," I said. At that he sat bolt upright, now wide awake.

"Nightmare?" he replied. "That was the most extraordinary dream I've had in my entire life." He then described his dream.

In the middle of the night James had woken to find a man standing by his hospital bed. The man had introduced himself as Professor John Kelly Reeves, who told him that because he did not have very long to live, he wanted to pass on some important information to James. He brought James to Newgrange, a prehistoric burial chamber situated north of Dublin in County Meath. He led him into the heart of the tomb, so that James's back rested on the stone slab which is touched by the first rays of sun each midwinter's day. The professor then led James forward out of the burial chamber, told him to turn left for a certain distance, then left again for another short distance, and finally left again. At this point James was instructed to start digging. "And you know, I discovered there the most wonderful thing. Buried under Newgrange I found this other pre-ancient city. I could see all the circular outline of the houses and the lines of the streets of this marvelous city as it spread out toward Dundalk. This is the treasure that I wanted to share with my sons."

I listened in awe as James recounted his dream. As he spoke he seemed to glow, and his physical frailty receded into the background. I congratulated him on having had such a wonderful dream. He was clearly delighted to be asked to go back over it as he clarified various details. He was himself surprised to have had such a dream and somewhat puzzled by its contents, because even though he knew of Newgrange he had never been there, nor read about it, nor previously had any particular interest in such things. I asked him to describe his feelings about the dream. "It was so vivid and real," he said, "but I wasn't frightened. It made me feel . . . famous." I repeated that it was great that he had had such a dream and been able to share it. "I hope something good comes of it," he replied.

Looking across the ward, James then told me that in the early part of the previous evening the man in the bed opposite his had died. He had cried, remembering his brother and sisters who had died in the previous months. He said he had various matters he needed to "sort out" and that he wanted to make a will. Finally, he concluded that meeting by declaring that he intended to put on "at least a stone weight" before he went home, and would like my help with this.

James died in the hospital less than two weeks after this. I met him on a number of occasions during that time. It was always a pleasure for me to visit him, and he too seemed happy to see me. It was as though his sharing his dream with me had created a bond between us. I usually began these visits by asking him how he was. He would then describe how he was feeling, and we would talk about what could be done to ease any discomforts he might have, which happily were few and minor at this stage. Invariably this part of the consultation ended with our discussing plans for his discharge home and our agreeing that he was not quite ready yet and that the hospital was the right place for him to be just then. He was obviously both content and relieved at this. At some stage in each of these meetings we spoke again about his dream. James always loved to do this, and as he spoke of the dream he appeared to change. It seemed that at such times he was fired with a quiet energy as he sat up, straight-backed, in the bed, speaking with a voice of calm authority.

Two days before he died, the occasion of my last meeting with him, he once again told me the dream in its entirety. When he finished, he mused on, looking straight ahead as he leaned forward and held his thin legs through the blankets. "You know . . . it was as though something struck me at one-thirty that morning . . . and what the professor said to me, maybe he meant that I didn't have very long to live? Anyway, I've lost my worries since that dream . . . I've been able to hand over my concerns to my sons . . . I was so frightened . . . I'm no longer afraid." Yet again, he ended that meeting by talking positively and hopefully about the future and his going home, "when the time is right." His final words to me were, "When I'm well enough, I'll take you to Newgrange. My son will drive us and I'll show you what I've seen."

I left James that day with some sadness, thinking that I would probably not see him alive again. In the corridor outside, one of his sons was waiting to speak to me. I told him that I felt his father's time was now very short. He replied that the family fully realized this and that, while they were very sad, they were doing all right. They were reassured to see James so comfortable and amazed at how peaceful he seemed to be despite his deterioration, in contrast to his agitation in the previous weeks. He died peacefully with his wife and two sons by his bedside later that evening.

By coincidence I made a first, long-planned visit to some Newgrange-type burial cairns in Loughcrew, County Meath, the following day. I thought of James as I sat in silence with my back against the stone at the heart of the tomb, and I sensed he was nearby.

I am occasionally asked, usually by a desperate patient, if I believe in miracles. The answer is yes, I do. Sometimes, I add, the miracle might not be quite as one expects, but yes, in my experience, they do happen. When I reply in this way I am thinking of someone like James.

Here was an ill, frightened man with just a couple of weeks left to live. Through his dream he had an experience which utterly transformed him. It was as if he were no longer trapped in a tight and fearful prison, as if, through the mediation of the dream, he had moved into depth and experienced a bigger place opening up to him.

In terms of the Chiron myth, although James's struggle was still there after the dream, evident in his continuing determination to put on weight and get home, it was no longer a desperate or central issue and became progressively less significant as he neared death. James had made a crucial choice; he had chosen to have faith in his dream. From here the dream took over with its own dynamic, carrying him into the healing power of dream-time. Hence his mellow calm in those final days, hence the sense of community and solidarity with the other men in his ward, hence the sadness of farewells as the new journey began, hence the synchronicity between his dream and my story and hence, and through it all, that golden light that filled him as on some midwinter's day.

I end this series of stories by telling of James and his remarkable dream because it seems to bring us full circle in its echoes of Bill's story, which I told in the first chapter of the book. For both these men, the extraordinary inner transformation they experienced shortly before their deaths appeared to happen quite spontaneously and did not result from any of the specialist interventions I have referred to as "depth skills." James's subsequent marveling at his dream echoed Bill's bemusement and pride that he should have such amazing wonders within himself. I find these stories particularly heartening, as they seem to confirm that whatever we do, or do not do, in our dying and in our working with those approaching death, there is another world and another work that wishes us and all our efforts well.

(Shortly after James's death, while reading about Newgrange, I came upon a reference to a John Rhys, an expert on the subject. He wrote a book entitled *Lectures on the Origin and Growth of Religion as Illustrated by Celtic Heathendom* [2nd edition, 1892]. I subsequently learned that a Professor John Kelley supervised the archaeological excavation of Newgrange in the 1960s. It is extremely unlikely that James heard of either John Rhys or John Kelley prior to his dream.)

PART 4

DEPTH WORK

Only the man who has raised his strings
among the dark ghosts also
should feel his way toward
the endless praise.

Only he who has eaten poppy
with the dead, from their poppy,
will never lose even
his most delicate sound.

Even though images in the pool
seem so blurry:
grasp the main thing.

Only in the double kingdom, there
alone, will voices become
undying and tender.

RAINER MARIA RILKE
(translated by Robert Bly)

The stories in this book suggest that as we face death, we need to attend not just to the outer but also to the inner aspects of the process of dying, or in the terms we have been using, to the deep as well as the surface aspects of our experience. They show that while the surface work is essential, it is only a beginning, and that the central issue is our relationship to depth and to soul. And while these stories show the extraordinary potential for personal growth and change at the very end of life, they also challenge us to find our own way of beginning to respond to the challenge of soul pain now, wherever and whoever we are.

As death approaches the quality of the time that remains becomes the issue. The stories I have shared show that this is determined by a dynamic interplay of a variety of factors, including aspects of the physical care these individuals received, the relationship between the individuals and their caregivers, and psychological changes within the individuals themselves.

First, the quality of the caregivers' skill was important. These individuals needed caregivers who were competent to deal effectively with their physical distress, who could sit and talk openly and clearly about what was happening, and who would spend time listening to their families' pain. They also needed these caregivers to be able to recognize the effort to palliate for what it was, an end in itself and the beginning of something else; a preparing and clearing of space in which the next phase of the story could unfold.

For these individuals the healing of soul pain came as they embarked on an inner journey in depth. While skilled and effective care was the essential first step in this process, the transforming descent into soul related more to the quality of relationship that was there between themselves and their caregivers. What mattered was not just what their caregivers did, but how they did it. What mattered was not primarily that the efforts of their caregivers were successful, but that they were prepared to stay with them, however things turned out. This brought the trust and security that allowed these individuals, in their own time and in their own way, to choose to let go to the unknown underworld within.

Finally, it is also clear from the stories that the human qualities of the caregivers themselves mattered. These individuals needed to have as a companion someone who was not afraid of the dark, someone who knew, from lived experience, what it meant to step into the unknown. This person did not need to "have it all sorted out," much less have all the answers, but needed to be able to live with questions and be committed to their own inner journey in depth. Such a person could recognize what was really happening for those dying individuals, could help them to realize that the way out was no longer by struggling to get away, and show them that they still had important choices to make. This person also needed to have the depth skills that were occasionally required to unblock what is normally a spontaneous process, so enabling the descent to continue. The individuals in these stories knew, without any words having to be spoken, when it was an apprentice to soul who sat beside them. Such a person brought them encouragement by their very presence, endorsing the words of the psalmist that "deep calls on deep, in the roar of waters."

Given the nature and cultural dimensions of soul pain, and acknowledging that our individual response to these issues is relevant, one central fact begins to emerge: each of us has to begin, again, to befriend soul. But where, when, and how might we act on this? The stories in this book point to the fact that there is just one place to start: with ourselves. By illustrating

the potential difficulties of leaving this until too late, they tell
us that the appropriate time to begin is now, and, by revealing
the disconnection at the heart of soul pain, they show that the
first part of this task is for each of us to consciously find our
own way of beginning a journey in depth.

> I have this that I must do
> One day: overdraw on my balance
> Of air, and breaking the surface
> Of water go down into the green
> Darkness to search for the door
> To myself in dumbness and blindness
> And uproar of scared blood
> At the eardrums. There are no signposts
> There but bones of the dead
> Conger, no light but the pale
> Phosphorus, where the slow corpses
> Swag. I must go down with the poor
> Purse of my body and buy courage,
> Paying for it with the coins of my breath.
>
> R. S. THOMAS, "This to Do"

Beginning a Journey
in Depth

It is hardly surprising that we need to look to other cultures for clues as to how we might begin this journey in depth. Buddhist traditions emphasize the value of daily exercises in death awareness, a form of meditative practice that consciously and regularly brings one from the surface to the deep. The teachings of the *Tibetan Book of the Dead* are intended to make the student so familiar with this process of threshold crossing and all the variety of associated experience that actual physical, bodily death when it does occur will have lost much of its sting. As the Buddhist teacher Sogyal Rinpoche puts it, "For someone who has prepared and practiced, death comes not as a defeat but as a triumph." Although less apparent, there are also western examples of this kind. It is interesting to note that a European version of death rehearsal exercises called the "Ars Moriendi" was still being widely practiced until the Middle Ages. It seems to have faded into the background as the achievements of "the age of enlightenment" came to the fore.

Tribal cultures also have much to teach us. In Australian aboriginal society, threshold crossings (for example, from childhood into adulthood) were, and still are, ritualized as initiation rites, the so-called rites of passage. The custodians of these rites are the tribal elders, who have themselves already been through the process of initiation. In externally ritualizing this move from the known to the unknown they are facilitating an inner transition from the surface to the deep levels of that initiate's experience. Repeatedly marking the process in this way enables

145

fear of the unknown to be tempered, again and again, by the discovery that there is life after death, a life which is always qualitatively different from life as previously known. This familiarity with threshold crossing, born of actual experience, will then be there as a rock to stand on when that individual comes to the final threshold.

If soul pain results from our being cut off from the deepest parts of ourselves, the wisdom of these other cultures points to the value of somehow finding a ritual way of crossing from the surface to the deep levels of our experience and of becoming familiar with depth. Each of us must find our own way of doing this. While for one it may mean learning the dream language of the soul and beginning the depth work of psychotherapy, for another it may mean a lifetime's dedication to a spiritual discipline or to one's art, or to working with the body in a way that acknowledges its wisdom and its kinship to soul.

For many the path into depth will be less formal and more about how they see and respond to the events that life itself is so generous in providing. The task then is to recognize such potential moments of initiation and to choose to cooperate with them. Danah Zohar describes such a moment in her book, *The Quantum Self*:

> During the pregnancy with my first child, and for some months after her birth, I experienced what for me was a strange new way of being. In many ways I lost the sense of myself as an individual, while at the same time gaining a sense of myself as part of some larger and ongoing process.
>
> At first the boundaries of my body extended inwards to embrace and become one with the new life growing inside me. I felt complete and self-contained, a microcosm within which *all* life was enfolded. Later, the boundaries extended outward to include the baby's own infant form. My body and my self existed to be a source of life and nurture, my rhythms were

those of another, my senses became one with hers, and through her, with those of others around me.

During all those months, "I" seemed a very vague thing, something on which I could not focus or grip, and yet I experienced myself as extending in all directions, backwards into "before time" and forwards into "all time," inwards towards all possibility and outwards towards all existence.

I joked at the time that I had lost my "particlehood" and my husband told me that I was experiencing projective identification with the baby. Freud would have called it an "oceanic feeling." Whatever, it was both unsettling and exhilarating and through it I lost my lifelong terror of death.

While for Zohar, pregnancy was the initiating life event which carried her into depth, for others it will be something very different. For many it will not so much be a dramatic epiphany as a gradual process resulting from a repetition throughout life and in many different shapes and forms of crossings from the familiar and the known to the unfamiliar and the unknown, not without fear, but with faith in life born of previous crossings. Zohar's account highlights that what is called for at such a time is a choice to trust and a conscious attention to the experience within the event. She describes the potential fruits of such discipline: new life and a falling away of fear.

There is a danger of sounding prescriptive or of identifying depth as some brave new world for the ego to colonize. Ultimately, it seems to matter less what particular path we choose into depth than what our attitude toward it is. It is not simply about moving into depth. This happens several times each day, such as in our moments of fantasy and daydream and each night as we enter the world of dreams. It is about doing this consciously, aware of the ritual dimension of such a move, aware also how we look at and appreciate the experiences that follow. Ultimately, it is about finding a right relationship to depth.

In this, we have much to learn from tribal cultures which have not lost their living connection with the soul of the world. To the Australian aboriginals, nature itself is a dreamscape, inhabited by the spirits and forms of the dreamtime, the very powers that keep the world in being. Their task is to find where they fit in this wider context. When they find their place the link is made, they sing their song, and the dream can continue. If we too are willing to accept that the depths have autonomy and that they may have something to teach us, then, I believe, we are in this "right relationship" and depth will respond. From that moment we become witness and apprentice, and depth becomes the teacher. And as we allow ourselves to be "done unto" by the depths, we too are being marked with the ochre-red paints of initiation and told new yet strangely familiar stories by the soul itself.

If the first danger was of sounding prescriptive, the second danger is of making it all sound too easy. We have seen in individuals' stories how the process of deep inner healing can be accelerated in those close to death. For those of us who choose to embark on this quest voluntarily and at an earlier stage of our life's journey, it does not appear to happen quite like this. This task is likely to take a lifetime of commitment and effort, with many false starts and disappointments along the way. What could possibly motivate us to persist with what can seem such a fruitless task? It is the sense of knowing, silent as the ground we walk on, that this is the way through to the heart of life itself. Whatever our life's work might be in a material sense, this journey into depth, this relationship with soul, will be our lifetime's inner work.

There are other dangers inherent to the journey in depth itself. As Jung puts it, "There are those who go digging for an artesian well and come instead upon a volcano." While the deep contains riches, treasures, and the potential for healing we must not forget that it is truly a place of power whose lower reaches are unfathomable. What maps we have of the underworld are at best rudimentary. There is a danger of getting lost in this place, of being devoured by its monsters or of being possessed by its energies, in short of entering the depths all right, but then failing to make the return part of the journey. The risks of being overwhelmed by the deep or unconscious mind are greatest for those who fail to honor this ancient place of power, for example by denying its very existence or by naively setting out to explore it alone. The risks are least for those who set out consciously and respectfully and, like the aborigine initiate, do so in the presence of an elder guide, one who knows the path from walking it smooth.

Wounded Healers

In the early part of the book, I presented the Chiron myth as a context for understanding the dying person's way into depth. This story also has something crucial to say about our own individual way through to depth and about the nature of the healing relationship.

At the end of the Chiron myth, the transformed centaur was immortalized as a constellation of stars in the heavens. This is another way of saying that the dynamic which is at the heart of the myth is eternally present and waiting, but normally out of reach. It is as though it takes life's incurable wounds, the hurts that cannot be made better, to constellate the Chiron dynamic in our own psyches, that is, to awaken its healing power in our own lives. It also indicates that our individual way into depth may not only be found in the place or way that we least expect, but that this way will, somehow, be inextricably bound up with that inner psychic wound that is uniquely ours and, ultimately, incurable. The Chiron myth reminds us that the very suffering from which we flee may be the gateway, the road, and the guide which can lead us through to the healing power of depth. I will try to illustrate what I mean here by sharing some of my own story.

Like Chiron I grew up either ignoring or devaluing what I have referred to as the "lower-half" values of body, instinct, feeling, and the imagination. For me what mattered was the intellectual life and a certain disembodied spirituality. As a medical student, circumstances brought me close to someone who was dying. After spending time with this person, I felt strangely comforted and noticed, over time, a strange yearning which led me to choose a career that would allow me to be with people close to death. It seemed that this yearning, this longing, was both satiated and increased by these contacts. I began to notice that, if it was allowed to do so, dying made these people more real, more human, and that in being close to them, I too felt more alive.

Over the years, I have taken time to reflect on this. This launched me on my own inner journey and led me to the encounters and insights I have shared in this book. It allowed me to recognize soul pain in others, because after many years in exile from soul, I knew this form of suffering intimately. It helped me to see that the process of dying itself midwifes a person into depth, and that the ensouling that is this healing is one that I too can know, as I stand alongside.

Who, therefore, is the healer in these encounters and who is the wounded one? We need to realize that Chiron's story is our story. As we reach out to the other who is dying, as we help that other person to move into depth, we are simultaneously reaching out to the one who is mortally wounded and suffering in the depths of our own being. At that moment we are not there as altruistic heroes helping the victim other. We and the other are both there as wounded ones, each searching for healing, and in this reaching out and reaching in we become wounded healers to self as we are wounded healers to other. Until we recognize this inner dynamic for ourselves, we will either mistakenly continue to believe that we as caregivers always have the answers to the other people's problems, or, as patients, continue searching in never ending circles for that someone or something "out there" who will at last take all our pain away. The tragedy in this is that we may never pause long enough to realize that the way to the healing we desire is, in fact, seeking us out, and always as close to us as we are to ourselves.

> We die with the dying:
> See, they depart, and we go with them.
> We are born with the dead:
> See, they return, and bring us with them.
> T. S. ELIOT

151

Build Your Ship
of Death!

D. H. Lawrence knew the depths of soul from years of inner travel. As a humbled apprentice he wrote:

> There is the other universe, of the heart of man
> that we know nothing of, that we dare not explore.
>
> A strange grey distance separates
> our pale mind still from the pulsing continent
> of the heart of man.
>
> Fore-runners have barely landed on the shore
> and no man knows, no woman knows
> the mystery of the interior
> when darker still than Congo or Amazon
> flow the heart's rivers of fulness, desire and distress.

Three years before he died, in April 1927 Lawrence visited Etruscan tombs in western Italy. In his book *Etruscan Places* he tells of his descent into these black burial caves with a friend and their guide. He describes the very act of entering these caves as a sort of symbolic dying and how, in the tomb of an Etruscan Lucumo or prince, he saw among the sacred treasures of the dead a "little bronze ship of death that should bear him over to the other world." This little bronze ship of death was to become the central image of one of his final poems, which he wrote as he lay dying of tuberculosis in the south of France:

We are dying, we are dying, so all we can do
is now to be willing to die, and to build the ship
of death to carry the soul on the longest journey.

What Lawrence calls "building a ship of death," and Hillman calls "soul-making," is spoken of in the East as building a "subtle" or "diamond-body." Each of these metaphors describes the task I have called depth work, and suggests that such work is more than a death rehearsal. I can only build my ship of death of soul materials, and so to build I must descend, again and again, becoming, as I do so, more and more used to being in the dark. On completion of the task, however, I am not only less frightened of the dark, I also have a "ship of death." I have a little vessel to carry that in me which does not die onto the waters of an unknown ocean:

Ah, if you want to live in peace on the face of the earth,
then build your ship of death, in readiness
for the longest journey, over the last of seas.

From descriptions of Lawrence's own death it seems that he suffered a lot of physical distress in his final weeks. He was in pain and short of breath but refused to take morphine to ease these symptoms until just hours before his death. Shortly before he died, he became fearful and said he did not know where he was, and called out for help. "If only I could sweat," he said, "I would be better." His lover, Frieda, sitting by the end of the bed, took his ankles in her hands. With this he settled and became calm. It was as though, in that gesture, he came home. His final words were, "I am better now."

What difference will depth work actually make to each of us when we come to die? I do not know. What difference did Lawrence's own building a ship of death make in and to his dying? I do not know. I am, however, silenced by echoes of his dying in lines from two of his poems, the second of which is believed to be the last thing he ever wrote:

Who is it smooths the bed-sheets like the cool
smooth ocean where the fishes rest on edge
in their own dream?

Who is it that clasps and kneads my naked feet,
     till they unfold,
till all is well, till all is utterly well? the lotus-lilies
     of the feet!

I tell you, it is no woman, it is no man, for I am alone.
And I fall asleep with the gods, the gods
that are not, or that are
according to the soul's desire,
like a pool into which we plunge, or do not plunge.

    *   *   *

Give me the moon at my feet
Put my feet upon the crescent, like a Lord!
O let my ankles be bathed in moonlight, that I may go
sure and moon-shod, cool and bright-footed
toward my goal.

The Chiron Myth*

Chiron was the son of the Olympian god Cronus and the earthly nymph Philyra. Cronus first came upon Philyra in Thessaly while searching for his baby son Zeus, whom his wife, Rhea, had concealed from him, weary of his repeated devouring of their offspring. Philyra changed herself into a mare to try to escape from Cronus, who was ardently pursuing her. However, Cronus in turn deceived her, by changing himself into a horse. Thus he succeeded in mating with her.

Eventually, a child of this union was born to Philyra. He was Chiron the centaur, who had the body and legs of a horse and the torso, arms, and head of a man. When Philyra saw the little creature waiting to be suckled she was filled with great loathing. She pleaded to be changed into anything other than what she was. The gods duly obliged by turning her into a linden tree. In this way Chiron was left an orphan.

Later, Chiron was found by Apollo, who took him into his care and became his foster father. Apollo was god of music, prophecy, poetry, and healing, a noble paragon of youth, beauty, wisdom, and justice. Chiron mirrored himself on Apollo who, in turn, educated him in all his ways.

Thus, Chiron became known as a wise man, a prophet, physician, teacher, and musician. His responsibility included the unruly centaurs themselves and various small kingdoms in northern Greece. Local kings entrusted their sons to him to be initiated into manhood and educated in the arts of leadership. He was teacher and mentor to many famous Greek heroes, including

*Adapted from *Chiron and the Healing Journey* by kind permission of Melanie Reinhart.

Jason, Achilles, Hercules, and Asklepios. His syllabus was broad and varied and included riding, archery, hunting, the arts of war and medicine, ethics, music, and natural science.

One day, the centaurs invited Hercules to dinner. A row erupted and Hercules began to fight them. As the centaurs fled in all directions, one of Hercules' arrows, poisoned with the blood of the Hydra, whistled through the air and stuck, quivering, in Chiron's knee. Because Chiron was a demigod, the poisoned arrow did not kill him. Instead, it created an agonizing and incurable wound. Hercules, repenting of this injury to his former teacher, drew out the arrow, and even though Chiron himself supplied the herbs for treating the wound, these were to no avail. Chiron retired, howling, to his cave.

Chiron suffered unceasing agony from this wound for the rest of his long life. He continued to search for a cure for the wound and, even though he was unsuccessful in this, he became increasingly knowledgeable in the healing powers of plants and his empathy grew for the sufferings of others. Even though he could not heal himself, Chiron became of ever greater help to others. In this way he became known as "the wounded healer."

One day, Hercules on his travels reached the Caucasian Mountains. There he came upon Prometheus, bound to a rock by Zeus in punishment for his mocking him and his theft of fire from Mount Olympus. Every day a griffin, a huge vulturelike bird, came and tore out Prometheus' liver, which then regrew at night, allowing the cycle of eternal torment to continue. Zeus had decreed that Prometheus could be released only if an immortal agreed voluntarily to go to Tartarus in his place, relinquishing his immortality. Hercules pleaded Chiron's case, and Zeus agreed to an exchange, if Chiron was willing.

When he took Prometheus' place, Chiron died and descended to Tartarus, where he spent nine days. Then Zeus intervened on Chiron's behalf and immortalized him as the constellation Centaurus. Hercules, invoking Apollo, shot the griffin through the heart.

An Analysis of the Chiron Myth: Wounding, Struggle, Choice, Descent, and Return

THE WOUNDING

Chiron's mother was mortal, a nymph called Philyra, while his father was Cronus, one of the gods. Because he was conceived while both his parents were in horse form, he was born a centaur, with a human head and torso and the body of a horse. The newborn creature was abandoned by both his parents but was adopted by the sun god, Apollo, who cared for him and taught him many skills. Chiron became a wise and respected teacher, and many future Greek heroes were among his pupils. One day, in the midst of a drunken brawl, he was wounded in the leg by a poisoned arrow fired from the bow of one of his prize pupils, Hercules.

THE PRIMAL WOUND

Chiron's primal wounding came through his abandonment by both his parents shortly after his birth, a rejection which left a deep if invisible mark. His foster father, Apollo, was renowned for his brightness, his activity, his fine intellect, and his mastery of many survival skills. Under Apollo's tutelage and encouragement, Chiron learned how to play musical instruments, began to write poetry, was taught the arts of prophecy, war, and medicine while simultaneously learning to read the stars and to become proficient at archery and hunting. It was as though the great sun god recognized Chiron's immortal spark and blew it to a mighty flame. It is also said that at this time Chiron discovered the medicinal properties of many plants. Before long his great wisdom and many skills became so famous throughout Greece that many rich and powerful kings entrusted their precious sons to him for their education and initiation into the mysteries of manhood.

The good in this is evident. Chiron was a sophisticated, wise, and just teacher, and some of his pupils were to become Greece's greatest heroes. What is also apparent is that in Chiron's success his primal wounding was forgotten. His early rejection was left far behind and far below as he ascended in ever higher spirals of activity. In this there was a complete denial of his "lower half." Because it was the reason for Chiron's being rejected by his parents at birth it is not surprising that he should have cut himself off from this part of himself and behaved as if it simply did not exist. But the denial was not just on Chiron's part. Apollo colluded with this. He particularly fostered his stepson's "upper half," the part that reflected his own sky-godly beauty. The only hint that this schism was incomplete comes in the detail that Chiron also discovered at this time the healing powers of certain herbs and plants. This was not an intellectual, rational, or scientific discovery but came as some half-awake reaching out of Chiron's instinctual animal nature.

Chiron's primal wounding is one that each of us shares. It represents the moment of betrayal that brings about our loss of innocence, that traumatic moment of rupture when we first discover that we live in an imperfect world. Whatever the individual circumstances, such a moment inevitably comes. The outer event which for some is horrific and explicit can for others be subtle and unseen. Invariably it is shocking and, as the protective bubble of innocence bursts, the hurt goes straight to the core.

THE MORTAL WOUND

As an adult Chiron was wounded for a second time. Unlike the primal emotional wounding, the wounding here was physical. More specifically it was to the lower half of his body, to his knee, where Hercules' arrow is said to have struck. The suffering Chiron experienced because of this was horrendous. The poison from the arrow, which was strong enough to kill any mortal, smarted and festered relentlessly in the wound. If Chiron had been merely mortal, death would soon have brought ease from his suffering. Instead, because he was half immortal, he could not die but was trapped instead with an unhealable wound in a prison of pain.

This mortal wounding brought Chiron's reluctant attention to his lower half. In contrast to his upper half, which revealed parts of himself that he liked and felt proud of, his lower half confronted him with parts of his nature that he deeply feared and had effectively disowned. As he looked at the gaping wound he saw, as if for the first time, something he had successfully managed to avoid all his life long: his body—the hairy, smelly, sweating body of a horse. With this, his primal wound was awakened. At that moment he saw himself as through his mother's eyes, and this acted like salt on raw flesh to increase his torment.

Both Chiron's parents were in horse form at the time of his conception. This is a way of saying that his horse's body represented all that was physical, sexual, and untamed in his nature. Centaurs were renowned for being disruptive and unruly, particularly after drinking wine. It was as though at such moments the animal part of themselves went wild and created havoc. Chiron had been particularly keen to carry on as though this part of himself did not exist.

Chiron's lower half, his horse's body, represents the instinctive and spontaneous side of our nature that runs free in the little child. On reaching "the age of reason" this part of ourselves is bound, gagged, and locked away in the darkness of the unconscious mind along with other parts of ourselves which we perceive as unacceptable to those around us. However, this solution, which may work well enough in the short term, is flawed for a number of reasons. Whatever is psychologically repressed is buried alive. As time passes it regresses, grows hairy and scary and becomes something we increasingly dislike and fear. Soon this part starts to look for a way out. It begins to wander through our nightmares, to slip out unnoticed in a cruel comment in the middle of a heated argument or, as with the centaurs, to break out in drunken violence. It can also somaticize as a physical symptom or illness. While this pattern of behavior is understandable, it is also potentially harmful, to ourselves and to others. It may also be short-sighted and wasteful. It is based on the assumption that these untamed parts of ourselves are wholly negative and dangerous and have nothing constructive to offer us. This assumption encourages us to alienate a part of ourselves that might also have something of value to give and teach us.

By denying his lower half, Chiron was cutting himself off from a profound and unrecognized potential. His denial represents a rejection of body and a rejection of soul. Until this moment Chiron had little regard for his body. While he was aware of its value as a frame to carry him about, he was more aware of its limitations, its needs to be fed and rested and its inability to keep pace with his flighty, tireless intellect. While he used his body, he did not see it as a valuable resource. He failed to recognize body as wise matter, body as link with the depths and treasures of the earth. He did not see body as teacher nor body as soul incarnate. And as he rejected the body, so he rejected the soul, the psyche, the anima, that in us which is experienced through emotion and a receptivity to image, dream, and symbol and the associative and intuitive aspects of the mind. Chiron did not see that in rejecting his lower half, he was, in fact, rejecting the very ground of his being. In this he failed to realize that in the dark earth of that ground, not far from the surface, lay a limitless and untapped vein of golden ore.

Finally, if Chiron's upper half and intellect connected him with his immortality, his animal body also connected him to that part of himself that he perhaps feared more than anything else, his mortality. Chiron was also mortal, but like all of us he preferred to listen to that in him which told him he would live forever.

THE STRUGGLE

Whereas to a mortal the wound would have been fatal, Chiron, because he was a demigod, did not die but was condemned instead to a tortured living death. He sought relief from his pain by trying countless different remedies, and although in the process he became wise in the use of healing herbs, his efforts were to no avail. Because of his wound and his generosity in sharing his wisdom with others, he became known as the wounded healer.

As well as bringing Chiron's attention to his lower half, his mortal wounding radically affected his behavior and his way of life. At first he reacted with that mixture of denial and hyperactivity which had served him so well until now. As previously every challenge had been a spur which had driven him on to ever greater achievements and to ever greater heights, he now set out confidently in search of a cure. He tried this remedy and that potion and sought advice and counsel far and wide but all to no avail. He could not accept his lack of success. Driven by this and his great pain he continued to struggle on, night and day, in his quest for the elusive balm.

As time went by, Chiron's life became different from before. Because of his damaged leg he could not travel far afield. Instead he wandered back and forth on the mountainside where he lived, or stayed in his cave alone. However, his pain did not diminish, and whenever he could he continued to search for a cure. Assisted by his daughter, Thetis, he limped through the neighboring hills, gradually getting to know the healing properties of each plant and herb. Instead of the wealthy sons of kings coming to be educated, those who now came to his cave were the sick, the lame, and the blind. They found him to be wise, saw that he had time to listen, that he had a wonderful knowledge of healing remedies but above all that he seemed to understand their sufferings with an extraordinary intimacy. Seeing his pain they were puzzled by his inability to help himself.

Chiron's struggle was an increasingly desperate attempt to find a way out of his prison of pain and suffering. It was also a struggle against the direction in which the wound was pulling him, which was toward his despised and feared lower half and the utterly unknown territory of his own mortality.

As struggle was Chiron's dominant behavior, so fear was the dominant emotion of this part of the story. But what did Chiron fear so much? While he may have entertained the idea of death as a possible "way out," it was also the source of his greatest terror. He feared the process of dying—that it would lead to even greater torments of pain, to dependency on others, to madness and isolation. And permeating and underlying all these specific fears was an existential dread of the utter darkness that is death.

The existential fear of death is there for a reason. A child who cannot feel such fear, like a child who cannot feel pain, will know no boundaries, for this fear marks the line between known and unknown territories. Such a child will wander unchecked from the safe and familiar to the unfamiliar and the unsafe, with potentially dire consequences. Such fear, therefore, has a protective function, signaling to us that we are approaching potential danger. It triggers a reaction of pulling in and back, of tightening and closing off to the experience at hand and of withdrawal to a safer place. Chiron knew such fear as the wound led him quietly and with a relentless gravity to a place he would rather not have gone, the line that marked the edge of the wound, the line that marked the threshold of the unknown.

While Chiron's heroic resistance to the downward pull of his wound did not have the effect he wanted, it was, nonetheless, an essential part of his healing and achieved a number of results which would otherwise have been unattainable. First, there might have been a way out. His struggle could have led to his emerging from the experience cured, as well as the wiser for it. Unless Chiron had struggled as he did, leaving no stone unturned in the process, he, and those close to him, would have had a lingering doubt about this. Second, the struggle brought him more fully into himself. It was as though until this moment he lived in only one small room at the very top of his house. Now, in his search for a cure, he opened the doors of all the other rooms on that floor and the floor beneath and the floor beneath that again, which brought him eventually to that heavily pad-locked and darkened door to the basement marked DANGER. By pushing himself to the limit of all his known inner resources he began to inhabit himself more completely. Third, Chiron's struggle slowed him down. One of the effects of a wound in the leg is a loss of mobility; another is a certain loss of indepen-dence. Chiron could no longer rush about in charge and in con-trol. Instead he hobbled through the hills, supported by his daughter. And as he slowed down and became acquainted with the experience of suffering, he became receptive and empathic, and this, even more than his increasing knowledge and skill in the use of herbs, was what made him a wise and compassionate healer.

Finally, as Chiron's futile struggle was preparing him for the next phase of his journey, it was simultaneously constellating the circumstances that would allow this to unfold. We are not told for how long he continued to struggle. The feeling one gets from the story is that it was for a very long time. He had tried and tried to find a way out. The desperation and fear of the early struggle had by then been permeated by a bone weariness and a growing desire to let go. It was at this moment that his wounder, Hercules, appeared back on the scene.

THE CHOICE

One day Hercules returned to Chiron and presented him with a possible way out of his suffering. Zeus had decreed that Prometheus, whom he had imprisoned for tricking and insulting him, could be released only if an immortal agreed voluntarily to surrender his immortality and offer himself in place of Prometheus. Chiron chose this path.

Eventually, the moment came, the timing of which was not in Chiron's control, when the possibility of release presented itself. But there was something utterly surprising and paradoxical about the circumstances of this. Help, when it did eventually arrive, came in the unlikely guise of the wounder; the path of healing he described sounded like a further wounding. At another time, such words would have added further torment to Chiron. However, by then he was ready. His years of suffering and struggle had prepared him to recognize such a sign. He did not want to hear this strange proposal, yet he knew immediately that this was the way through he had been seeking.

No matter how long and how hard Chiron tried, he could not have done it all on his own. Hercules' reappearance in the story at this stage indicates that in a situation such as this, an additional approach to that of the individual's own heroic efforts may be needed, not to do the work for that person but to point to another possible way through. It also seems relevant that Hercules was acting here out of compassion and atonement for his old teacher and in service and on behalf of Zeus.

There is also the aspect of the timing of such an intervention. Somehow the years, the months, the weeks, the days, and even the seconds of Chiron's seemingly futile struggle against his unwanted fate had been the necessary path to that inner place where Hercules found him receptive to the message he brought. When Hercules arrived, Chiron was ready; ready to let go. Because the timing was right, Chiron could recognize the opportunity in Hercules' message.

"HE WHO WOUNDS, HEALS"

Hercules, Chiron's wounder, now became his healer, and the healing path on offer was that Chiron now consciously entered the dark abyss of his mortal wound. The appearance of irony and paradox in the story marked Chiron's arrival at the threshold of a new territory. His back was now to that place he had come from, where all was either black or white, good or bad, yes or no, one thing or the other, and his face looked toward a new world, home of seemingly irreconcilable opposites, where polarities and contradictions coexisted side by side.

Hercules' arrival also presented Chiron with the opportunity to radically review his predicament and, indeed, the very nature of heroism. Until now, heroism meant to fight, resist, and struggle against the pain, and not to count the cost. This version of heroism had by then achieved all it could for Chiron. Hercules' proposal acknowledged that this way was now redundant and suggested that the new heroism was to choose one's fate, to say yes to what was already happening, to go with the pull of gravity, to dive even as the waters pulled one under.

"QUICK NOW, HERE, NOW, ALWAYS"

The choice which Hercules presented to Chiron was a stark one. It meant saying yes to what he had been fighting against all these years, it meant saying yes to the process which began the moment the arrow struck his leg, and it led to one remaining certainty—that death awaited him.

Chiron's unconditional "yes" had irreversible and radical consequences. There was the immediate loss of his immortality and the inflationary sense that he could be his own redeemer. Instead of struggling vainly if valiantly to control his own destiny, he had now begun to cooperate with the forces that shaped it. At that moment Chiron was transformed from tragic victim to courageous seeker, one prepared to plunge into the abyss of the unknown in search of healing. While he would still have heard the desperate voice of fear, Chiron may now have noticed a new voice starting to come through—a voice as old and silent as the stars.

Chiron knew at that moment that he was utterly alone and that he was naked as the day he was born. With this came a new way of seeing his mortal wound. What had been the source of endless and meaningless torture became instead the gateway to healing. With this came a lessening of his pain as the particular torment of struggling against the inevitable waned with an awareness that even though he neither liked nor wanted what was happening, he was unexpectedly back on course; he was on his way through.

PROMETHEUS

Chiron's choice led to the freeing of Prometheus, who, like him, had up until then also been a prisoner of pain.

In Greek mythology, Prometheus, a Titan, was seen as the creator and champion of humanity. He is said to have formed mortal men from clay and water in the likeness of the gods, whereupon the goddess Athena breathed life into them. When Athena taught Prometheus architecture, astronomy, mathematics, navigation, medicine, and other useful skills, he immediately passed these on to his beloved human creation.

One day a dispute arose as to which portion of the sacrificial bull should go to the gods and which should be reserved for men. Prometheus, acting as arbitrator, tricked Zeus into choosing the bones of the animal and laughed behind his back. Zeus was furious at this and punished Prometheus by withholding fire from mankind. "Let them eat their flesh raw!" he cried. Prometheus, with Athena's help, gained access to Mount Olympus, where he stole fire from the furnace of the gods and brought this to mankind. When Zeus discovered this he swore revenge. Through Pandora he sent the Spites to mankind; old age, labor, sickness, insanity, vice, and passion. Meanwhile, Zeus had Prometheus chained naked to a pillar in the Caucasian Mountains, where a vulturelike griffin tore at his liver all day long, year after year. By night, while Prometheus was exposed to frost and snow, his liver grew whole again, and so each dawn heralded another day of agony.

By the time Hercules came to the Caucasian Mountains, Prometheus had been a prisoner there for thirty thousand years. When Zeus had agreed to Hercules' plea to release Prometheus only if he could find an immortal willing to let go of his immortality and go to Tartarus in place of Prometheus, Hercules remembered Chiron.

As a result of Chiron's choice, Prometheus was freed. This was on condition that he wear forever a willow wreath on his head and a ring on his finger, fashioned from the chain that had been binding him and set with a stone from the rock to which he had been bound. The willow was associated with Hecate, one of the goddesses of the underworld, and Prometheus' agreeing to wear the wreath may be seen as a sign of his acceptance of mortality. The ring was a reminder of his period of captivity and the need for humility in his future dealings with the gods.

Chiron's choice was, therefore, also a sacrificing, that is, a "making holy" of all that Prometheus symbolized. If previously Prometheus was champion of a humanity in competition with the gods, after his release he stood for humanity in all its creative autonomy but now allied to an awareness of its mortality and with humility toward the gods. This is a mythological way of describing the change that comes about as persons who are "patient" cease, when the moment is right, to struggle against the wind, who turn their small sailboat around and allow the wind to fill their sail and carry them where it will.

THE DESCENT

And so Chiron died and descended to Tartarus.

Chiron's descent did not begin at the moment of his choice. It began at the moment of his wounding by the poisoned arrow. With his choice to swap places with Prometheus, what changed was the rate of descent. The spiral of descent now accelerated, utterly beyond his control. Furthermore, the experience of descent would have had for Chiron a déjà vu quality. He would have experienced his abandonment as a tiny child as the loss of his world, as a death of self. And so he would have experienced the descent as being at once strangely familiar and utterly new. While the familiarity was in the fact that he had been thrust this way before, the newness was that, on this occasion, he was making the descent by choice.

To where and to what did Chiron descend? He descended to the ancient Greek underworld called Hades, which is also the name of the god who ruled there. Unlike the narratives of underworld journeys of certain other mythical characters, there is no detailed account of Chiron's descent to Hades. We can, nonetheless, imagine what might have happened.

Chiron would have entered through the main gateway to the underworld, which was said to lie in a grove of black poplars beside the ocean. As he traveled downward, he would, like all souls making this journey, have been guided by Hermes, the god of betwixt and between, who was unique among the deities in his ability to travel between worlds. He would soon have arrived at the river Styx, whose name means "hatred" or "hateful" and whose frozen waters marked the boundary of Hades' kingdom. To cross Styx Chiron would have had to pay Charon the faceless boatman, who carries his passengers only one way.

On arriving on the opposite shore Chiron would have encountered Cerberus, the ferocious three-headed dog, whose task it was to devour any living intruders or ghostly fugitives. He would then have passed through the sullen, silent, and gray Asphodel fields where the throngs of the dead, twittering like bats, awaited judgment.

Before long he would have arrived at the Palace of Hades and Persephone, the queen of the underworld, and encountered nearby the three judges who would have decided his fate. From this place of judgment Chiron would have passed down one of three roads. The first, for those judged neither virtuous nor evil, led back to the Asphodel fields. The second, for those judged virtuous, led to the orchards of Elysium, which was a happy place of play and pleasure and eternal day and whose inhabitants could choose to be reborn on earth whenever they wished. The third road, for those judged evil, led to Tartarus. While it is evident that Chiron would not have been judged evil, we also know that Prometheus' release was conditional on an immortal's going willingly to Tartarus in his stead. While Tartarus was sometimes used interchangeably with Hades as a name for the whole underworld, it also described a particular region of that shady place. So Chiron's descent may not have ceased until he eventually found himself in Tartarus, the farthest, deepest, blackest chasm of the underworld.

HERCULES IN HADES

The stories of Chiron and of Hercules, the ultimate Greek hero, interweave at several significant points. Just as Apollo became step-father to Chiron, so Chiron in turn adopted the young boy Hercules. Hercules became Chiron's finest pupil, outstripping all others in bravery and strength. As an adult Hercules was set a series of twelve apparently impossible "labors," which he was instructed to complete by the gods, through the Delphic Oracle. This was to atone for the horrific damage he had inflicted during an episode of madness and to attain the prize of immortality. It was in the course of completing the Fourth Labor, the capture of the Erymanthian Boar, that Hercules unwittingly inflicted the mortal wound on Chiron. Many years later, as he was returning through the Caucasian Mountains, having successfully completed the Eleventh Labor of fetching the golden apples of the Hesperides, he came upon Prometheus bound in chains. This reminded Hercules of another in eternal torment, and he intervened with Zeus to barter for Chiron's release in place of Prometheus. While, until now, Chiron and Hercules shared a common bond of allegiance to the heroic approach, it was in their starkly contrasting ways of descending and being in the underworld that this bond was broken as they went two very different ways.

Chiron's descent followed the choice on his part to let go of his immortality on behalf of Prometheus. In this he was also letting go of the heroic dynamic which had dominated his life until then. His attitude to the underworld was not one of a hero who had come to take, but of a novice and apprentice who had come with all to learn, who had no expectations of what this would lead to. His release and reward followed and flowed from this receptivity and the unconditional willingness on his part to be initiated by depth into its mysterious ways.

In stark contrast, when Hercules descended into Tartarus to complete the twelfth and final labor, he did so as heroic colonizer. His task was to capture the fierce three-headed watchdog of the underworld, Cerberus. Hercules, armed with a sword and bow and arrows, went down to take him. He did not believe the words whispered to him by one of the ghosts, "You have nothing to fear from the dead." Instead, he reacted to what he saw and met as he would have in the upper world. He slaughtered cattle, wrestled with a herdsman and, in echoes of his early wounding of Chiron, shot an arrow into Hades' shoulder.

Cerberus belonged to Hecate, who was a goddess in the underworld and a close friend of the queen of the underworld, Persephone. While the Hellenic Greeks who told this story had begun the process of demonizing Hecate by portraying her as a dark witch, she is, in fact, thought to represent the pre-Hellenic triple goddess who ruled the upper world, the seas, and the underworld prior to being deposed by the arrival of the patriarchal trinity of Zeus, Poseidon, and Hades. Traces of this earlier version of events are seen in the detail that Zeus granted Hecate the power of bestowing on mortals the gift of what they most desired. In this light Hercules' brutal capture and abduction of the triple-headed dog can be seen as a further attack on the power of the triple goddess by the heroic principle. Hercules' way, the heroic way of being and acting in the underworld, is nothing less than the rape of the feminine principle and a plundering and desecration of soul.

In psychological terms, Hercules in Hades is a description of the potential damage the heroic ego, that aware and organizing part of our mind, can inflict on the deep, inner world of soul. There are other accounts of Greek heroes descending into Tartarus, but each of them had previously been initiated into the Eleusinian Mysteries, which meant that they had been educated in the otherworldly ways of the underworld and so descended in humility. Even though Hercules underwent initiation into the Lesser Eleusinian Mysteries, his destructive behavior in the underworld suggests that the initiation never took effect. The Herculean way of descent is seen in certain psychological techniques which access the image-laden depths of soul with the purpose of gaining better understanding and more control of one's life. Ultimately, this is about ego-strengthening at the expense of soul and does not bring inner healing. It results in the caricature of humanity which Eliot depicts in his image of "The Hollow Men":

> We are the hollow men
> We are the stuffed men
> Leaning together
> Headpiece filled with straw. Alas!
> Our dried voices, when
> We whisper together
> Are quiet and meaningless
> As wind in dry grass
> Or rats' feet over broken glass
> In our dry cellar
>
> Shape without form, shade without colour,
> Paralysed force, gesture without motion;
>
> Those who have crossed
> With direct eyes, to death's other Kingdom
> Remember us—if at all—not as lost
> Violent souls, but only
> As the hollow men
> The stuffed men.

Chiron is one of those who had "crossed with direct eyes, to death's other kingdom." In psychological terms this represents the descent of the ego that respects depth. For each of us mortals, as was the case for Chiron, the preparatory Eleusinian Mysteries that bring this humility are the unavoidable encounters with incurable physical or emotional suffering which life brings our way. This means that when our ego eventually descends it does so under no illusions of grandeur. In depth, this receptive and patient ego can then be transformed into what Hillman calls "the imaginal" or "dream-ego," and return from the deep, unconscious mind to the waking, conscious mind, transformed and capable of seeing and acting in a new way.

Chiron's way of descent describes those psychological approaches which regard the deep mind as having in it elements that are autonomous and primary. Here depth is not simply viewed as a psychic dustbin for repressed memories and emotions. Rather it is seen as our guide and advocate, whose generous images can direct our life from below. What matters then is not that we succeed in pinning down these images as we might a butterfly in the gallery of our understanding, but that we learn to trust them and enable them to live, that we allow them to underpin and understand us and to infuse our waking lives with their resonant, wise, and loving ways.

DESCENT AS SHAMANIC INITIATION

As the Chiron myth is a relatively contemporary, western reworking of the universal theme of shamanic initiation, the significance of Chiron's descent to the underworld can usefully be examined in this context.

The shaman, whose role combined that of priest and physician, has been at the center of tribal cultures since the Paleolithic era and the dawning of human consciousness some two hundred thousand years ago. Shamans continue to play a crucial role in certain tribal societies where this lineage remains intact. A common belief of these tribal societies is that not only the well-being but the very survival of individuals, of the tribe itself, and of the planet depends on an interconnectedness and harmony of these different parts. This interconnectedness describes not only a networking and interdependency of these various elements but also, at a microcosmic level, a healthy dynamic interplay between different planes of consciousness within that individual. The shaman is one who, because of his initiation into mystery, can travel to other levels of consciousness and experience. He can access the underworld of ancestral spirits, the worlds of the vital forces of nature and animals, and the planes of being of the deities on whom life depends. Because of this ability to access and mediate between these different parts of the overall picture, the shaman is seen within the tribe as an essential linking strand in the web of life.

There are a number of discrete stages to the shaman's initiation process, the first two of which are relevant here. First, there is the "crisis." One does not decide of one's own volition to become a shaman. Rather it is a vocation, where the initial "calling" comes, as for Chiron, with the initiates' receiving an incurable wounding of a physical or emotional nature, which plucks these individuals out of everyday life, pulling them inward and downward to the melting pot at the center of themselves. What follows is the second stage of the initiation process, which appears to the bystander as a period of sickness or madness, when the initiate may seem to be on the very threshold of death or, at times, to have actually crossed over. While this is happening, an intense inner journey is also underway, with the initiates traveling downward to the very core of their being. This phase of the process, when the initiate neither experiences nor is guaranteed any future beyond this immediate experience, has obvious parallels with Chiron's descent into and sojourn in Tartarus.

UNDERWORLD AS OTHERWORLD

Chiron's descent into the underworld of death, with its echoes of shamanic initiation, describes an experience that is utterly new and radically other. While his host, Hades, was renowned for his hospitality and was also known as Pluto, meaning "rich one," the underworld was not all sweetness and unrealized treasures. Chiron had traveled down to a level that was far below the fruitful black earth, to the lowest parts of the underworld, to Tartarus, that place of utter and unchanging darkness and cold unmoving depths. His fellow inhabitants, the dead, appeared as "shades" who were said to have wandered "bodiless, bloodless, and boneless" and who spoke in whispers. Chiron had traveled into depth, he had arrived in the autonomous kingdom of soul, that place where images live, move, and have their being, and for all he knew at that moment, this is where he was to stay.

The change in the focus of Chiron's attention from his upper to his lower half followed by his death and subsequent descent to the underworld can also be seen in metaphorical terms. As such it describes a move from the upper world of consciousness, rational analysis, and linear thinking to the dark, intuitive, and image-laden depths of the unconscious mind. The cold, implacable, and hateful nature of the river Styx, with its one-way ferry service, is a reminder that such a crossing is neither pleasant nor easy and explains the desperate fear and resistance of the heroic ego to such a move, which it rightly sees as a kind of death. This is the death that occurs each time we "fall" asleep. This is the death that occurs each time we enter the irrational world of art, poetry, and religious experience. This is the death that occurs each time we cross into natural wilderness and experience ourselves as no longer lord of all we survey, but as one tiny part of a vast and unknown landscape. What Chiron's story seems to say is that whether we want to or not we will all, one day, make this transition and that just as our initial struggle against it is valuable, so, at some point in the process, is our choice to cooperate with the pull of its gravity. This then brings us into dreamtime, into the cold and other world of depth, where like children in a pitch black room we need to allow our pupils to dilate slowly, we need to learn to wait.

THE RETURN

After nine days in Tartarus, Zeus set Chiron's image among the stars as the constellation Centaurus.

As Chiron stood, a newcomer in that cold and dark place, his first experiences were of blindness and bewilderment. There were also feelings of sadness as he remembered what he had left behind. Then, gradually, as his eyes adjusted to the dark, he began to see the outlines of this other world. He started to wander through the black labyrinthine tunnels, trying to get his bearings and hoping to see a chink of light, some tiny spark of encouragement. Before long he found himself back where he began, and this was the result no matter how often or how hard he tried. And even though he was now in an utterly new location, there was a strange sense of familiarity to his wanderings. With the shock of recognition he suddenly realized that what was familiar was not the place but the pattern of his activity. Once again he was engaged in a futile struggle to find the impossible. With this he tumbled deeper still, into a black and bottomless ocean of hopelessness.

Chiron gradually began to realize that nothing needed to be done, because nothing could be done. With this he experienced a growing sense that something in himself had to change. He needed to recognize that he was no longer the master, no longer the teacher. He needed to accept that the old world order had been turned on its head and would never be the same again. He needed to see that now he was the novice, and underworld was teacher.

Chiron's first lessons involved developing a new attitude to depth and learning how to wait. In the past Chiron had either feared or totally disregarded what was not in the domain of reason. Now, as he gazed about the underworld, he thought he noticed the faintest glimmer of gold in the rock before him and he remembered that Hades' other name was Pluto, meaning "the rich one." He was once again confronted with a choice.

Would he let himself drown in the black sea of hopelessness that surrounded him on every side, or would he put his faith in the possibility that even in this there was an intelligence that wished him well? Chiron chose the latter, and his ability and willingness to wait in that place came from this new attitude.

The way Chiron learned to wait is described by T. S. Eliot in *Four Quartets:*

> I said to my soul, be still, and wait without hope
> For hope would be hope for the wrong thing; wait
>   without love
> For love would be love of the wrong thing; there is
>   yet faith
> But the faith and the love and the hope are all
>   in the waiting.

And as he waited, allowing that he might be in a place of wisdom, something strange began to happen. At first the moving shades barely caught his attention. They appeared bloodless and uninteresting, and their movement seemed illogical and chaotic. However, with time he began to find himself attending to their musings more closely. Although he could neither understand their language nor their actions, he began to feel that they had significance. This sense of significance was a very different thing from that clear analytical insight for which he had been renowned during his life in the upper world. Here was something emotional and physical rather than intellectual, something that touched him in the pit of his stomach, filling him with a wordless sense of meaning. Chiron was being initiated into the mysteries of depth. As with any initiation, it involved listening to stories of the new world he now inhabited, which tasted like an unfamiliar but delicious food to his starving soul.

How long Chiron waited and listened and learned in the underworld nobody knows. The story tells us that he was in

Tartarus for "nine days." But what does time mean in this time-less place? Perhaps there are clues in the fact that nine is a sacred number signifying wholeness and completeness. In addition, it may be significant that although Tartarus is a tomblike place, nine also numbers the months mortals spend enwombed. What seems important is that Chiron waited in Tartarus until such time as he had learned what he had to learn. This was when Zeus decided to intervene on his behalf. As far as Chiron was concerned he might have been there forever. The reprieve, when it came, was a completely unexpected surprise. The first he knew was that he was moving upward, not of his own power but somehow carried by the power of the stories he had heard and the visions he had seen. As Chiron rested in the heavens, he saw the happenings of the upper world in a new way. His waiting continues, eternally.

UNDERWORLD AS INITIATOR

Chiron's waiting in the cold and utter blackness of Tartarus echoes the shamanic initiate's incubation in the crisis of physical or mental sickness. During that time, which can last from hours to days or even weeks, the initiate appears to the onlooker to be very gravely ill. Simultaneously, deep inside, the initiate is experiencing other levels of reality. This is sometimes described in terms of a "flight" or a "night sea journey," equivalent to Chiron's "descent to the underworld." This is what Eliade describes as a "breakthrough in plane," meaning that the initiate has crossed the threshold from the normal mode of waking consciousness to a deeper, more intuitive and image-laden level of mind.

What the initiate experiences next varies enormously from individual to individual. For some it is pleasant, for others not so. For all it is utterly other and unexpected. What seems to be happening is that all ties between that person and their former life are being severed. They then pass into the giant melting pot of the psyche, where all that previously was is dissolved back to its basic chemistry, like a pupa in the chrysalis. Many describe this afterward as an experience of total body dismemberment. This is truly an experience of "being done to" by the depths and parallels Chiron's time of receptive and unconditional waiting in Tartarus. And just as Chiron had no power over his fate at this point, so what happens next is not for the initiates to decide. One possibility is that the initiate may not make the return but may actually die or linger on in a state of serious illness or madness. The other is that after some time, as long as it takes, the initiate does come back, but as a changed person.

The initiate's return depends, in terms of the Chiron myth, on whether, when, and how "Zeus intervenes." In the shamanic process this intervention is called the moment of "solarization" or "universalization of consciousness." What this describes is the initiates' arrival at their deep inner center, that essential place which is at once intensely personal and continuous with the transpersonal. How significant is the initiate's role in this happening? In considering Chiron in Tartarus, it was evident that even though he did not have power to control events around him, he did have choice as to what attitude he would adopt toward them. It was Chiron's willingness to surrender to the wisdom of the depths that enabled his initiation to begin, an initiation which culminated in Zeus's intervention. I suspect that this is so for the shamanic initiate as well. *How* we wait in that place does seem to be crucial, for, to quote Eliot again, "the faith and the love and the hope are all in the waiting."

The moment of solarization, just like the intervention of Zeus, cannot be prescribed. All that can be "done" in anticipation of such a moment, like the builders of the passage graves of old who placed their stones and waited in midwinter, is to create the space and wait for the sun's return. For that is what we are talking about here; that column of light piercing the dark heart of the tomb is the moment which some call "grace." This moment, then, is not so much a matter of the initiate's finding the deep center, as this implies that it is simply a matter of their having to try a little bit harder. Rather, it is a matter of the initiate's being found by the deep center, for, as the North American Indian saying goes, "It is not for us to stalk the vision, the vision is stalking us."

It is from this experience that the initiated shaman returned. As he opened his eyes and looked up from the sickbed, he recognized where he was and the anxious faces that looked down on him, and he knew that because of what he had just experienced, life would never be the same again. Before he had descended into the crisis of his initiating illness, "family" meant the flesh and blood connections with these people now surrounding him. In his journey to the center, these ties had melted away like gossamer thread in flame. He was now returning not of his own power, but carried like an eagle on the rising warm air from the molten deep center of being. This connection to the deep center linked the initiate to the stars in the dark cosmos and to the love that held all things in being. And it was from this connection to the core of being that he now related. Each person around him, whether familiar to him or not, as each tree and rock and pool and creature, was now brother or sister. He returned as one humbled by the mysteries and as one in service; in service to the transcendent and in service to his earthly family. His task was now to link the creative powers of the world of depth to the daily life of the community in which he lived.

THE MYSTERY OF TOUCH

D. H. Lawrence's fatal illness was his mortal wound, his initiatory crisis, and his final poems carry the authority of one who is talking from the depth of such experience. In "Bavarian Gentians" the dark blue flowers lying on a table in his room become a gateway to depth. He writes:

> Reach me a gentian, give me a torch!
> let me guide myself with the blue, forked torch
>   of this flower
> down the darker and darker stairs, where blue
>   is darkened on blueness . . .

Through the long and painful personal struggle of his terminal illness, Lawrence had come to a point where, like Chiron presented with the choice of exchanging places with Prometheus, he could recognize the gentians as a doorway to depth and the path he was longing to take. In the rough draft of this poem, he wrote:

> How deep I have gone
> dark gentians
> since I embarked on your dark blue fringes
> how deep, how deep, how happy!
> What a journey for my soul
> in the blue dark gloom
> of gentians here in the sunny room!
>
> . . . .
> it is dark
> and the door is open
> to the depths.
>
> it is so blue, it is so dark
> in the dark doorway
> and the way is open
> to Hades.

Lawrence continues:

even where Persephone goes, just now,
    from the frosted September
to the sightless realm where darkness is awake
    upon the dark
and Persephone herself is but a voice
or a darkness invisible enfolded in the deeper dark
of the arms Plutonic, and pierced with the passion
    of dense gloom,
    among the splendour of torches of darkness,
    shedding darkness on the lost bride and her groom.

The image of Persephone, queen of the underworld, being ravished by its king, Pluto, echoes Zeus's intervention on Chiron's part or the shamanic initiate being found by the deep center. It describes the receptivity to miracle that is the end and the beginning, and it hints that the fruit of this experience will be child to the divine. These lines are a celebration of the nourishing and healing power of darkness. They are the song of one who has come through and whose soul thrills in the blue-black depths.

Lawrence summarizes this whole process in two short poems. In "Full Life" he describes the ruthless and unconditional letting go involved:

> A man can't fully live unless he dies and ceases to care,
> ceases to care.

In "Initiation Degrees" he speaks of the cost of this letting go and its potential consequences:

> No man, unless he has died, and learned to be alone
> will ever come into touch.

In psychological terms, what is on offer here is not, as might seem to be the case at first glance, a prescription for a self-centered and callous existence. Lawrence is saying that unless we move below the everyday level of reality with its personal ties, and spend solitary time in the deep inner spaces of who we are, we can never know the meaning of real love. The mystery of touch tells of intimacy and of separate body meeting separate body. Like Chiron eternally present, like the Shaman among his community, touch is the divine child and the fruit of the return.

Afterword

The importance of this book lies in the power of Dr. Kearney's approach to the problem of suffering as a prelude to death, especially that soul-driven agony of body and mind which is Western civilization's peculiar contribution to human misery. Compassion has led Kearney to a solution in terms of the innate human capacity to experience the immaterial roots of self-awareness— call it the level of self, soul, or what you will—and so to receive the reassuring touch of what does not die, and with it the sense of a meaningful existence.

Experience of this level takes one to a vantage point which literally provides a new world view with practical consequences. Viewed from that vantage point, the appreciation of pain may change to such an extent that the dosage of drugs required to control it may be reduced to a half or less.

Kearney's approach is independent of religious doctrine, though in no sense antagonistic to it; yet he is aware that his method is rooted in antiquity—in the early Shamans, for example, whose spontaneous psychic powers and their perceptions in some sense guaranteed the reality of their experience of the inner worlds. Their discipline was so demanding that they themselves had had to "die a little," thus putting them in a position to help others die and to find healing in the acceptance of death.

The method described here, which is often so effective at the approach of death, has developed out of secular psychology and is known as imagework. Those who experience it in the agony of their pain and fear and denial may find their remaining days changed: pain becomes more bearable; hopes, fears, and worries lose their power to dominate the mind; and relationships improve.

If this is not religious, neither is it some new stunt of psychotherapy. It is reminiscent of the Upanishadic verse which describes the very beginnings of the spiritual quest: "Some wise man, seeking what does not die, with inturned gaze beheld the Self." That was neither mythology nor religious doctrine. It was a real man seeking a real answer to the emptiness of existential meaninglessness, seeking and finding at the very root of his being.

So the book is much more than a message of hope for those who are dying in pain. It is an invitation to die a meaningful death with dignity by virtue of finding one's self-identification with what does not die.

What a pity it is that these small but highly significant exercises in self-discovery must wait for the last days of terminal illness, when pain is the spur to try anything that promises relief, instead of being seen as part of a lifelong preparation for entry into a meaningful existence.

Sri Madhava Ashish

(Sri Madhava Ashish is a Hindu monk of Anglo-Irish-Scottish descent who lives in an ashram in Mirtola, a remote area in northern India.)

Bibliography

Achterberg, J. *Imagery and Healing—shamanism and modern medicine.* New Science Library, 1985.

Assagioli, R. *The Act of Will—a guide to self-actualisation and self-realisation.* Turnstone, 1984.

Berndt, R. M. and C. H. *The World of the First Australians.* Aboriginal Studies Press, 1988.

Bly, R. *A Little Book on the Human Shadow.* Harper and Row, 1988.

Bosnak, R. *A Little Course in Dreams.* Shambala, 1986.

———. *Dreaming with an AIDS Patient.* Shambala, 1989.

Campbell, J. (editor). *The Portable Jung.* Penguin, 1976.

Callanan, M., and P. Kelley. *Final Gifts—understanding and helping the dying.* Hodder and Stoughton, 1992.

de Chardin, P. T. *Activation of Energy.* Collins, 1970.

De Foucauld, C. *Come Let Us Sing a Song Unknown.* Dimension Books.

Edinger, E. F. *Ego and Archetype.* Shambala, 1992.

Eliade, M. *Shamanism—archaic techniques of ecstasy.* Arkana, 1989.

Eliot, T. S. *Collected Poems, 1909–1962.* Faber and Faber, 1963.

Feinstein, D., and P. Elliott Mayo. *Mortal Acts—eighteen empowering rituals for confronting death.* Harper San Francisco, 1993.

Frankl, V. *Man's Search for Meaning—an introduction to logotherapy.* Hodder and Stoughton, 1987.

Glouberman, D. *Life Choices and Life Changes through Imagework—the art of developing personal vision.* Unwin, 1989.

Grail Translation. *The Psalms.* Fontana, 1966.

Graves, R. *The Greek Myths: 1 & 2.* Penguin, 1990.

Grof, S. *Books of the Dead.* Thames and Hudson, 1994.

Grof, S., and J. Halifax. *The Human Encounter with Death.* Dutton, 1977.

Halifax, J. *Shaman—the wounded healer.* Thames and Hudson, 1982.

Hannah, B. *Encounters with the Soul: active imagination, as developed by C. G. Jung.* Sigo Press, 1981.

Hillman, J. *A Blue Fire: selected writings by James Hillman.* Edited by Thomas Moore. Routledge, 1990.

———. *The Dream and the Underworld.* Harper and Row, 1979.

———. *Re-Visioning Psychology.* Harper and Row, 1975.

———. *Suicide and the Soul.* Spring Publications, 1976.

Jimenez, J. R., and F. G. Lorca. *Selected Poems,* translated by Robert Bly. Beacon Press, 1973.

Jung, C. G. *Foreword and commentary, The Secret of the Golden Flower, a Chinese book of life.* Translated by Richard Wilhelm. Arkana, 1984.

———. *Memories, Dreams, Reflections.* Recorded and edited by Aniela Jaffe; translated from the German by Richard and Clara Winston. Flamingo, 1983.

Kreinheder, A. *Body and Soul—the other side of illness.* Inner City Books, 1991.

Kübler-Ross, E. *On Death and Dying.* Macmillan, 1969.

Martin, P. M. *Experiment in Depth—a study of the work of Jung, Eliot, and Toynbee.* Routledge and Kegan Paul, 1955.

Meier, C. A. *Healing Dream and Ritual.* Daimon, 1989.

Mindell, A. *Coma—key to awakening.* Shambala, 1989.

Moore, T. *Care of the Soul—how to add depth and meaning to your everyday life.* Piatkus Books, 1992.

Lawrence, D. H. *Complete Poems.* Penguin, 1993.

Levine, S. *Who Dies?—an investigation of conscious living and conscious dying.* Gateway Books, 1986.

Reinhart, M. *Chiron and the Healing Journey—an astrological and psychological perspective.* Arkana, 1989.

Rilke, R. M. *Selected Poems,* translation from the German and commentary by Robert Bly. Harper and Row, 1981.

Rinpoche, S. *The Tibetan Book of Living and Dying.* Random House, 1992.

Saunders, C., and N. Sykes. *The Management of Terminal Malignant Disease.* Edward Arnold, 1993.

Thomas, D. *Collected Poems 1934–1953.* Everyman, 1988.

Thomas, R. S. *Collected Poems 1945–1990.* Phoenix Giants, 1993.

von Franz, M. L. *On Dreams and Death.* Shambala, 1986.

Wheelwright, J. H. *The Death of a Woman.* St. Martin's Press, 1981.

Zohar, D. *The Quantum Self.* Flamingo, 1991.

Index

189